Book Synopsis

"*Spirits That Attack Dance Ministers & Dance Ministries*" is designed to teach and equip dance ministers and ministries with discerning and overthrowing the wiles of the enemy as he strives to steal, kill, and destroy the fruit and progress of dance ministers and dance ministry teams. This book will reveal the hiding oppositions of the devil, where for years he has wreaked havoc in the ministry of dance, and hindered the fullness of God's excellence, character, and culture from being the fruit of dance ministry. It will also equip dancers and ministries in being able to discern and identify specific spirits and attacks, when they are attacking your entire team or individual members, how to walk with team members in deliverance and healing, while process them to wholeness, and how to conquer these attacks with sustaining victory. Receive from this arsenal of revelation and powerful applicable knowledge, while being enlightened to dance ministry, intercession, warfare, and regional influence that will tremendously advance and supernaturally SHIFT your dance ministry and the atmospheres you minister in.

(Website) Kingdomshifters.com

Connect with Taquetta & Nina via Facebook or YouTube

Copyright 2016 – Kingdom Shifters Ministries

All rights reserved. This book is protected by the copyright laws of the United States of America. This book may not be reprinted for commercial gain or profit. The use of occasional page copying for personal or group study is permitted and encouraged. Permission will be granted upon request.

Taquetta's Bio

Taquetta Baker is the founder of Kingdom Shifters Ministries (KSM). She has authored fourteen books and two decree CD's. Taquetta has a Master's Degree in Community Counseling with an emphasis on Marriage, Children and Family Counseling, a Bachelor's Degree in Psychology and Associates Degree in Business Administration. In addition, Taquetta has a Therapon Belief Therapist Certification from Therapon Institute and has 22 years of professional and Christian Counseling experience.

Taquetta is also gifted at empowering and assisting people with launching ministries, businesses and books and provides mentoring, counseling and vision casting through Kingdom Shifters Kingdom Wellness Program. Taquetta serves on the Board of Directors for New Day Community Ministries, Inc. of Muncie, IN. In October 2008, Taquetta graduated from the Eagles Dance Institute under Dr. Pamela Hardy and received her license in the area of liturgical dance. Before launching into her own ministry, Taquetta served at her previous church for 12 years. She was a prophet, pioneer and leader of Shekinah Expressions Dance Ministry, teacher, member of the presbytery board, and overseer of the Altar Workers Ministry. Taquetta receives mentoring and ministry covering from Bishop Jackie Green, Founder of JGM-National PrayerLife Institute (Phoenix, AZ), and was ordained as an Apostle on June 7, 2014.

Taquetta flows through the wells of warfare and worship and mantles an apostolic mandate of judging and establishing God's kingdom in people, ministries, communities, and regions. Taquetta travels in foreign *missions and throughout the United States. She has mentored and established dance, altar workers, deliverance, and prophetic ministries. Taquetta ministers in the areas of fine arts, all manners of prayer, fivefold ministry, deliverance, healing, miracles, atmospheric worship, and empowers and train people in their destiny and life's vision.*

Connect with Taquetta and KSM at <u>kingdomshifters.com</u> or via Facebook. For more information regarding Bishop Jackie Green at Jgmenternational.org

Nina's Bio

Nina Cook has been saved since childhood and has been active in ministry much of her life. Nina carries an apostolic mantle with giftings in dance, singing, production, all manner of prayer, spiritual warfare, deliverance, healing, teaching, pastoring, scribing, and wellness. Nina graduated from Ball State University in 2014 with a Bachelor's Degree concentration in Exercise Science and a Minor in Dance. Nina has over 5 years of experience in the wellness and exercise field and 11 years of dance experience.

Nina is an Elder at Kingdom Shifters Christian Empowerment Center in Muncie, Indiana. She is the main armor bearer for her pastor and is also training in her calling as an apostle. Nina is the founder of "Manifold Grace Production Company" and "Exercise to Life." It is her vision that her production company brings transformation to people and regions through the power and creativity of the arts. Nina is an extraordinary teacher and minister of movement, choreography, atmospheric worship, and using dance and movement in warfare and intercession. Nina provides fitness coaching and exercise and dance class through "Exercise to Life." She utilizes a vast variety of exercise and fitness styles that people can do that are combined with scriptural focuses, short teachings, prayers, and declarations and decrees such that when people do the exercises their bodies are transformed. It is her vision to see people transformed through bringing healing and deliverance to the physical body in areas that hinder their health and wellness, and to also see complete lifestyle changes that shift people into wholeness.

Nina is dedicated to living her life sold out to Christ. She is generally the first to volunteer and take risks for anything that grows the kingdom. She is always seeking to learn, develop, and cultivate herself in the integrity, character, fruit and will of God.

Connect with Nina and Manifold Grace Production Company and "Exercise to Life" at kingdomshifters.com or via Facebook, and Youtube.

Table Of Contents

Keywords To Dismantling Strongholds................1

Discerning of Spirits...3
Spiritual Cleansing..7

Spirits That Attack Dance Ministers & Dance Ministries...29

Spirits That Attack Identity............................34
* Shyness..36
* Fear...37
* Condemnation...38
* Inadequacy & Low Self-Esteem...............39
* Rejection...40
* Pride..41
* Lust...42

Spirits That Attack Practice & Engagements........47
* Deaf and Dumb Spirit...............................47
* Zapping Spirit..49
* Cloaking Spirit...50
* Blocking Spirit...52
* Python Spirit..53
* Spirit of Leviathan...................................54
* Mind Binding & Blinding Spirit..................55
* Spirit of Void & Darkness........................56
* Little Girl, Little Boy Spirit.......................60
* Inadequacy, Insecurity, & Low Self-Esteem......62
* Spirit of the Outcast................................63
* Outcast Youth...67
* Controlling Spirits....................................71
* Spirit of Intimidation................................75
* Spirits of Rebellion, Stubbornness, Defiance.....76
* Spirits of Murmuring & Complaining...................81
* Spirits of Competition & Comparison..................83

* Mocking Spirits..87
* Spirit of Pride..92
* Spirit of Betrayal..95
* Spirit of Performance & Entertainment............100
* Spirit of Offense..104
* Spirit of Defense...108
* Spirit of Perfection......................................111

Spirits That Attack Dance Mantles & Callings........115
*Jealousy Spirits Operating in Dancers & Dance Ministers... 115
* Spirits of the Copycat as it Relates to Dance Garments...116
* Spirits of the Copycat as it Relates to Dance Styles..123
* Spirits Using Dance Teams to Attack One Another...129
* Mocking & Perverse Spirits that Defame Dance Ministry..132
* Spirits of Affliction That Attack Dance Ministers.137
* Spirits of Sickness & Infirmity That Attack Dance Ministers..144
* Sickness That Manifest as Words of Knowledge & Revelation...147
* Kingdom Vision for Dance Ministries................149
* Covenant Impartations......................................158

Maturity In Your Gifting & Calling........................161

Nuggets for Dance Ministers & Ministries............165

KEY WORDS TO DISMANTLING STRONGHOLDS

As you partake of the revelation in this book, it will be important to know a few key words that may be utilized to explain demonic forces, and how they operate. Those words are as followed:

> *Ephesians 6:12-13* For we wrestle not against flesh and blood, but against principalities, against powers, against the rulers of the darkness of this world, against spiritual wickedness in high places. Wherefore take unto you the whole armour of God, that ye may be able to withstand in the evil day, and having done all, to stand.

- **_Demons_** are demonic forces, evil spirits or devils that possess, oppress, torment or influence a person, place, or thing.
- **Principalities** are satanic princes and territorial spirits ruling over a nation, city, region, and community for the purposes of establishing Satan's demonic plan in people's lives and spheres.
- **Powers** are high ranking supernatural demons or demonic influences that cause evil and sin in the world.
- **Rulers of Darkness** are demonic forces that govern deception and manipulative hardships and catastrophes that are generally produced by witchcraft, manipulation of the weather and worldly systems; they operate in cultures and

countries such that idolatry and sin rein in the earth.

- **Spiritual Wickedness in High Places** are evil plots and deceptions, and demonic attacks directed in and against the church and God's people for the purposes of hindering, contaminating and demolishing God's will in the earth.
- **Strongholds** are demonically possess, demonically depressed, demonically griping clutches, barriers, or entanglements that harass, influence, hinder and/or prevent a person from being free to walk in the full salvation for the Lord.
- **Conjure** is utilizing demonic spirits, demonic influences, witchcraft, magic, and curses to produce supernatural effects.
- **Holy Spirit** is God's spirit in us.

DISCERNING OF SPIRITS

Sometimes demonic spirits can operate within dance ministers, among a dance teams and within an atmosphere and territory/region of a ministry. These demonic spirits will oppress, depress, negatively influence, possess or stronghold the communication, interaction, unity, personality, attitude, progress, effectiveness of the ministry team or team members.

The manner in which these demonic spirits attack are as followed:
- **Oppress** -to burden, restrain, weigh heavy upon, to put down; press down, subdue or suppress an atmosphere or the soul, heart, body of a person.
- **Depress** - to make sad or gloomy; lower in spirits; deject, dispirit, to lower in force, vigor, activity, etc.; weaken, make dull, a person or atmosphere.
- **Negatively influence** - cause confusion, discombobulation, double mindedness, unexplainable weariness, tiredness or sluggardness, irritation, frustration, ungodly thoughts, and thought racing within a person or atmosphere.
- **Possess** - to occupy, dominate, or control a person or atmosphere.
- **Strongholds** are demonically possessed, demonically depressed, demonically griping clutches, barriers, fortresses or entanglements that harass, influence, hinder and/or prevent a person from being free to walk in the full

salvation of the Lord (2Corinthians 10:3-5, Ephesians 4:22-23, Matthew 16:19, Mark 3:27).

Because we are all working out our salvation, demons can be intertwined in a person's soul, heart, mind, and body. They can also be intertwined within the personality of a person, which can sometimes cause them to go unnoticed. This being the case, it is not always obvious that a demon is at work in a person's life.

> **1John 4:1-2** *Beloved, believe not every spirit, but try the spirits whether they are of God: because many false prophets are gone out into the world. Hereby know ye the Spirit of God: Every spirit that confesseth that Jesus Christ is come in the flesh is of God.*

<u>Try</u> in the Greek is *dokimazō* and means:
1. to test (literally or figuratively); by implication, to approve, allow, discern, examine
2. to test, examine, prove, scrutinize (to see whether a thing is genuine or not)
3. to recognize as genuine after examination, to approve, deem worthy

Whether a person is good or bad, our friend or our enemy, our family member or a stranger, we have the right to try their spirit at any given time to examine if they are operating in the Holy Spirit, a Demonic Spirit or a Human Spirit:

- ❖ **The Holy Spirit** is God's spirit living inside of us (John 14:26, Acts 1:8 Romans 8:26, Galatians 5:22-23, Isaiah 11:12).
- ❖ **Demonic Spirit** are demonic forces, evil spirits or devils that possess, oppress, torment or influence a person, place, or thing (1Peter 5:8, Revelation 16:14, Ephesians 6:10-18, 1Corinthians 11:14, Mathew 12:43-45, Matthew 13:22).
- ❖ **Human Spirit** is in operation when a person is ruled or driven by his or her will, soul and/or heart desires or by the flesh (Hebrews 4:12, 1Corinthians 2:14, Jude 19, Romans 8:16).

We try every spirit using the gift of discerning of spirits found in ***1Corinthians 12:10***:

> *To another the working of miracles; to another prophecy; to another discerning of spirits; to another divers kinds of tongues; to another the interpretation of tongues.*

Discernment in the Greek language is *diakrisis* and means *"judicial estimation, discern, disputation."* It comes from a word meaning to separate thoroughly, withdraw, oppose, discriminate, decide, hesitate, contend, make to differ, doubt, judge, be partial, stagger, waver. So if you wrestle with wavering in what you discern, now you know why. These words describe the process the receiver of discernment goes through! When the discerner is confronted with something that appears good on the outside, but is not, it becomes a stumbling block to his spirit. His flesh sees good signs, but his spirit is disputing, opposing, hesitating, contending, differing, doubting, staggering, and wavering against the outward appearance. Discernment is an internal war as one grapples to line up what they perceive, with who God is, and what is being offered.

Matthew 15:26 lets us know that deliverance is the children's bread. That means believers can have demonic spirits and that deliverance is for the believer. We are exposing these demonic forces not to embarrass people or for leaders and members to be rebuking one another. The purpose is so we can more adequately discern how demonic forces are infiltrating our lives, practices, and ministries to undermine and lessen our effectiveness, unity, progress and maturity in the call and gifting of dance ministry. The more discerning we are, the more we can:

- Free ourselves and atmospheres of these demonic forces
- Mature in operating and manifesting the pure power of God
- Unify as an effective praise and worship army of God

This book will provide balanced wisdom on how and when to confront and/or be delivered from these demonic forces.

SPIRITUAL CLEANING! MAINTAINING DELIVERANCE & HEALING

This book will not only discuss the spirits you will be overthrowing, but will provide tools and strategies for sustaining your freedom, while learning to live a lifestyle of wellness with God. This chapter will provide you with knowledge of some of the strategies and tools that will be listed throughout this book. You shall be fully armored to break the power and stronghold of the devil as your revelation and arsenal becomes empowered with truth and weaponry to dismantle, seize, and invalidate the enemy. **SHIFT!**

> **Matthew 10:8** *Heal the sick, cleanse the lepers, raise the dead, cast out devils: freely ye have received, freely give.*

<u>Leprosy</u> in the Greek is *leora* and means:
1. scaliness, i.e leprosy
2. the most offensive, annoying, dangerous, cutaneous disease
3. the virus of which generally pervades the whole body, common in Egypt and the East

<u>Cleanse</u> is *katharizo* in the Greek and means:
1. make clean, cleanse
    a) from physical stains and dirt
        - utensils, food
        - a leper, to cleanse by curing
        - to remove by cleansing

- b) in a moral sense
  - to free from defilement of sin and from faults
  - to purify from wickedness
  - to free from guilt of sin, to purify
  - to consecrate by cleansing or purifying
  - to consecrate, dedicate
2. to pronounce clean in a Levitical sense

Leprosy is an infectious disease that causes disfiguring sores, nerve damage, and progressive debilitation. In the bible, lepers, or those infected with leprosy, were outcasts because of fear and necessity. Leprosy has the potential to spread from person to person. If lepers were not isolated, then they were a threat to society due to contaminating others with leprosy.

Lepers are also isolated due to how others react to them. The manner in which the disease physically alters a person, and the fear others had regarding how lepers looked, and fear of contracting what they had, were factors in them being in isolation.

> ***Leviticus 13:45-46*** *And the leper in whom the plague is, his clothes shall be rent, and his head bare, and he shall put a covering upon his upper lip, and shall cry, Unclean, unclean. All the days wherein the plague shall be in him he shall be defiled; he is unclean: he shall dwell alone; without the camp shall his habitation be.*

> ***Numbers 5:1-3*** *And the LORD spake unto Moses, saying, Command the children of Israel, that they put out of the camp every leper, and every one that hath an issue, and whosoever is defiled by the dead: Both male and female shall ye put out, without the camp shall ye put them; that they defile not their camps, in the midst whereof I dwell.*

Though the bible does not makes this clear, leprosy was viewed as God's wrath and judgment on a person's life due to sin. God may not have caused people to have leprosy, however, the manner to which leprosy would affect our lives is the same way sin affects our lives. Let's take a moment to explore the comparison:

- Sin causes us to be unclean, impure, and unhealthy.
- Our sin contaminates and influence others; it pollutes society and the world at large.
- We think people cannot see our sins, but sins can be seen in our presentation, disposition, personality, clothing, conversation, perceptions, communication, interactions, relationships, how we handle situations, and how we live our lives (out of our heart flow the issues of life ***Proverbs 4:23***).
- Sin outcasts us from God's presence and his plan for our lives.
- Sin defames God and tarnishes his reputation, especially when we are living a life of sin, but contend we serve God.

When we consider the concept of cleansing the lepers or shall we say, cleansing sins, it is important to cleanse out the infection and cleanse what is causing the infection.

> *Matthew 8:1-4* *When he was come down from the mountain, great multitudes followed him. And, behold, there came a leper and worshipped him, saying, Lord, if thou wilt, thou canst make me clean. And Jesus put forth his hand, and touched him, saying, I will; be thou clean. And immediately his leprosy was cleansed. And Jesus saith unto him, See thou tell no man; but go thy way, shew thyself to the priest, and offer the gift that Moses commanded, for a testimony unto them.*

A lot of times, we want to use will power to stop sinning. When using will power we are operating through a well of self-control. We are striving to control our impulses and choices. But if we could not keep ourselves from engaging in the sin, how can we stop ourselves from never doing it again?

We need Holy Ghost power.

> *Ephesians 3:16* *He would grant you, according to the riches of His glory, to be strengthened with power through His Spirit in the inner man,*

God's Holy Ghost power empowers us to grow strong, so we can withstand against sins and worldliness.

> ***The Amplified Bible*** *May He grant you out of the rich treasury of His glory to be strengthened and reinforced with mighty power in the inner man by the [Holy] Spirit [Himself indwelling your innermost being and personality].*

Even if you use your own will to stop sinning, you are still unclean if you do not allow God's Holy Ghost power to cleanse you from sin.

In ***Matthew 8:1-4***, Jesus laid hands on the lepers and they were made clean. This is miraculously awesome and is a form of deliverance and healing that many of us have experienced when encountering Jesus. Even with this miraculous cleansing, the leper still had to make a lifestyle change to remain clean.
- He could not return to the leper camp as he would risk being contaminated again.
- If his leprosy was a sin issue, then he had to reframe from that sin to maintain his deliverance and healing.
- Even as the leper's community had changed, his relationships and interactions had to be changed.

The leper's identity and lifestyle had to change to maintain his healing. Such a change requires a processing to wholeness. This requires relationship with God beyond just the initial encounter of deliverance and healing. We have to journey with him in a lifestyle change, learn his plan for us in maintaining healing, and walk that plan out in our daily lifestyle.

This brings us to this scripture:

> **Isaiah 64:6** *But we are all as an unclean thing, and all our righteousnesses are as filthy rags; and we all do fade as a leaf; and our iniquities, like the wind, have taken us away.*

<u>Unclean</u> is *tame* in the Hebrew and means:
1. to be unclean, become unclean, become impure, regard as unclean
2. to be or become unclean, to defile oneself, be defiled
   - sexually
   - religiously
   - ceremonially
   - by idolatry
3. to profane (God's name)

<u>Filth</u> is *ed* in the Hebrew and means:
1. to set a period, the menstrual flux, soiling, filthy
2. menstruation
   - a filthy rag, stained garment
   - figuratively of best deeds of guilty people

> **The Amplified Bible** *For we have all become like one who is unclean [ceremonially, like a leper], and all our righteousness (our best deeds of rightness and justice) is like filthy rags or a polluted garment; we all fade like a leaf, and our iniquities, like the wind, take us away [far from God's favor, hurrying us toward destruction].*

Even our righteousness needs cleaning in God's eyes. Just like we cleanse our physical body, we have to cleanse our hearts, minds, thoughts, souls, and the inner man of things lodged in our flesh. When we cleanse our physical bodies we are detailed in making sure we clean every part of our bodies. We even purchase the correct hygienic products to assist us with cleaning our bodies, while making sure we remain clean. And if a product does not work, we do not keep using it. We will try different products until we find out what products work best in keeping our bodies clean, vibrant, and fresh.

We need this same standard for our spiritual lives. And seeming even our righteousness is filthy, we should be cleaning our soul, hearts, minds, and our inner man daily just like we do our physical bodies. For even when we think we are clean, to God we have things that we need to be cleansed from.

Let's explore the Holy Spirit equipping you with healing techniques you can use to bring cleansing to your life:

- **Infilling of the Holy Spirit** (*Acts 1-2, Acts 13:22 And the disciples were continually filled with joy and with the Holy Spirit*). All of us receive the Holy Spirit upon us when we accept Jesus as our personal savior. When I speak of infilling, I am referencing speaking in tongues where God's voice and power speaks through you and empowers you. When God's power flows through you, his voice equips you with greater heavenly sound and power to annihilate the enemy. There are somethings the enemy will not respond to in your voice, but he will if you speak in tongues. If you do not speak in tongues, begin to study the purpose of doing so, while asking the Holy Spirit to manifest his voice through you. If you do speak in tongues, practice praying in your prayer language for at least 30 minutes a day. I encourage people to speak in tongues the entire time they are in the shower or while they are driving to work. This is the perfect time because you are generally alone and can focus on allowing the Holy Spirit to empower you. You do not have to know what you are saying or even have a prayer focus. The more you speak in tongues, the more you will know what you are saying and the more the Holy Spirit will guide you in knowing what to pray for, against, and how to use your prayer language to cleanse yourself of the filth of the enemy.

- **Spirit of Lord** – empowers you with the revelation, knowledge and guidance needed to handle your daily affairs and journey in a destiny lifestyle with the Lord. (*Isaiah 11:2 And the spirit of the LORD shall rest upon him, the spirit of wisdom and understanding, the spirit of counsel and might, the spirit of knowledge and of the fear of the LORD*). Declare continually that you are consumed in the spirit of wisdom, understanding, etc. Refuse to accept and cleanse out all confusion, ignorance, foolery, witchcraft, bewitchment, mind control, mind blinding/binding, lack of knowing, lack of guidance, etc. while asserting your right to have the spirit of the Lord teach you all things (*John 14:26 But the Comforter, which is the Holy Ghost, whom the Father will send in my name, he shall teach you all things, and bring all things to your remembrance, whatsoever I have said unto you*).

- **Blood of Jesus** – purges, purifies, redeems, reconciles, sanctifies, sanitizes, forgives, heals, frees you from death (*Ephesians 1:7 whom we have redemption through his blood, the forgiveness of sins, according to the riches of his grace*). We hear a lot about pleading the blood but the blood is an application. Jesus applied his blood to our sins and sicknesses, and through his perfected blood, we were redeemed and made whole. You can apply the blood of Jesus to your soul, heart, mind, thoughts, personality, character, righteousness, body, and command redemption, life and wholeness to come. You can soak yourself in the blood until you see breakthrough in these areas or as a daily application of being cleansed and free in God.

- **Binding, Loosing & Casting Out Devils** – delivers you from demons, and strongholds (*Matthew 16:19 And I will give unto thee the keys* *of the kingdom of heaven: and whatsoever thou shalt bind on earth shall be bound in heaven: and whatsoever thou shalt loose on earth shall be loosed in heaven*). You possess the power to bind up demons and demonic kingdoms, cast them out of yourself and others, and release the kingdom of God in your life, atmosphere, and region. You can also loose yourself from demonic powers and since binding, loosing and casting are keys, you can seek the Holy Spirit on how to use these weapons to be delivered from the enemy.

- **Fruit of God** – fills, restores, produces, reproduces (***Galatians 5:22-23*** *But the fruit of the Spirit is love, joy, peace, long suffering, gentleness, goodness, faith, Meekness, temperance: against such there is no law*) Cleanse yourself of all defiled fruit that does not represent the character and nature of God, while filling yourself up in all of the fruit that represents his character and nature.

- **Breaking Curses** – provides personal, generational, regional, cultural freedom from negative words spoken over you or curses implemented due to personal and generational sins (***Galatians 3:13*** *Christ hath redeemed us from the curse of the law, being made a curse for us: for it is written, Cursed is every one that hangeth on a tree*).
    - Repent for personal, generational, regional and cultural strongholds

- Loose the blood of Jesus to cleanse the curse and all filth associated with it
- Bind and cast out any spirits operating with the curse
- Declare your freedom through Jesus Christ (**2Corinthians 3:17** *Now the Lord is that Spirit: and where the Spirit of the Lord is, there is liberty*).
- Fill yourself back up with the fruit of God

- **Word of God** – discerns, divides what is of God and what is not of God, cuts out, does surgery, in stills God's truth, will, and plan (**Hebrews 4:12** *For the word of God is quick, and powerful, and sharper than any twoedged sword, piercing even to the dividing asunder of soul and spirit, and of the joints and marrow, and is a discerner of the thoughts and intents of the heart*). Use the word of God to overthrow every lie that the enemy uses to keep you bound to demons. Use the word of God to cut out any word, character trait, hurt, pain, and flaw that keeps you bound to demons. Spend time studying, meditating on, and soaking yourself in the word of God. Allow God's word to go inside of you (heart, mind, soul, identity), and cleanse out everything that is contrary to the word of God for your life.

- **Fire of God** – burns out, fuses, refines, purges, purifies, consumes, and test (**Malachi 3:2-3** *But who may abide the day of his coming? and who* *shall stand when he appeareth? for he is like a refiner's fire, and like fullers' soap: And he shall sit as a refiner and purifier of silver: and he shall purify the sons of Levi, and purge them as gold and silver, that they may offer unto the Lord an offering in righteousness*). Sometimes you will cast out demons, but their deposits and attributes are still lodged in you. Use the fire of God to purge and burn out these demonic deposits. You can also purify and refine yourself with the fire of God. Demons hate the fire of God and the blood of Jesus. Fire is judgment to demons. You can use the fire of God to torment demons and send them fleeing from your life (**Revelations 20:10** *And the devil that deceived them was cast into the lake of fire and brimstone, where the beast and the false prophet are, and shall be tormented day and night for ever and ever*).

- **Fullers' Soap** – is a washing by trampling, treading, stamping, scrubbing. It is liken to trampling or scrubbing something hard until it is clean. (**Malachi 3:2-3** *But who may abide the day of his coming? and who shall stand when he appeareth? for he is like a refiner's fire, and like fullers' soap: And he shall sit as a refiner and purifier of silver: and he shall purify the sons of Levi, and purge them as gold and silver, that they may offer unto the Lord an offering in righteousness*). When there are things in you that require deep cleansing, use the fuller soap of God to scrub it out.

- **Power of God** – delivers, overthrows demonic powers and governments, releases the virtue and government of God, releases miracles, signs, and wonders (***Acts 1:8*** *But ye shall receive power, after that the Holy Ghost is come upon you: and ye shall be witnesses unto me both in Jerusalem, and in all Judaea, and in Samaria, and unto the uttermost part of the earth*). Use the power of God to annihilate the powers of the enemy (***Luke 10:19*** *Behold, I give unto you power to tread on serpents and scorpions, and over all the power of the enemy: and nothing shall by any means hurt you*). Study the power of God as you will find that you have the ability to recreate and create body parts, birth forth things that you need, bring excellency to your heart, mind and soul, release virtue into your life, such that it brings deliverance and healing.

- **Glory of God** – refreshes, fulfills, establishes relationship with God, instills God's character, nature, truth, knowledge, revelation, pleasures forevermore (***Psalms 16:11*** *Thou wilt shew me the path of life: in thy presence is fulness of joy; at thy right hand there are pleasures for evermore*). You should be living inside the presence of God. This is where your direction of life is revealed. As you walk in alignment with God, continual fulness of joy and pleasures of God should be evident in your life. If you live in the glory of God, you should be living a fulfilled life no matter what trials and tribulations may occur. Ask God for revelation on how to build a relationship with him where you abide in his presence. Use his presence to refresh, fulfill, and fill you. Continually cultivate your life and atmosphere in his presence so you can be a true glory carrier (*John 15:4 Abide in me, and I in you. As the branch cannot bear fruit of itself, except it abide in the vine; no more can ye, except ye abide in me*).

- **Rivers of Living Water** – stirs, replenishes, breeds life, vitality, beauty, youthfulness, creativity, strength, efficiency, releases what is inside of you to whatever you are sending it to (*John. 7:38 He that believeth on me, as the scripture hath said, out of his belly shall flow rivers of living water*). It is important to spend time cleansing out the rivers that are inside of you, such that the wells that you flow out of, are pure as whatever is in you will be released to those you minister to.

- **Pluck Out** – roots out, pulls down, destroys, throws down (*Jeremiah 1:10 See, I have this day set thee over the nations and over the kingdoms, to root out, and to pull down, and to destroy, and to throw down, to build, and to plant*). Some spirits and demonic attributes are imbedded in your foundation and need to be uprooted. You can command demons and strongholds that are lodged deep within you to come up out of you by the root. That root can even be generational so keep that in mind, or it can be a root in you that has been there for years. You may also have to pull down something such as pulling down strongholds, imaginations, prideful spirits, that have exalted themselves above God and may have even exalted themselves as idols in your life. You cannot be nice to demons and with wickedness. Your mission has to be to destroy them just like they want to destroy you. The devil understands he is in a fight and will throw you around like you are a piece of paper. You have to enter your fight with him and be willing to toss him and trample on him as if your life depended on it – because it does. Use the power and authority of God to uproot, pull down, destroy and throw down.

- **Hammer Down-** walls have to be hammered down (***Jeremiah 23:29*** *Is not my word like as a fire? saith the LORD; and like a hammer that breaketh the rock in pieces?*). Sometimes these walls are made by us, sometimes the words and ideologies of others cause these walls and barriers, and sometimes they are made by the devil. Either way they need to come down. Use the hammer of God to break down walls and barriers that have been erected to hinder your breakthrough.

- **Run Through Troops** – blast through groups of troops that keep you bound or that may be blocking your breakthrough (***Psalm 18:30*** *For by thee I have run through a troop; and by my God have I leaped over a wall*). If you read Psalm

18:30-51, you will discern that it is the power of God that enables you to do this. When you find yourself ganged up on by demons or you come up against a stronghold that does not want to budge, ask God to empower you to run through troops. Then use your faith, power and authority to blast through these bondages.

- **Resist the Devil** – stand against, oppose, withstand, set against the devil and all that concerns him (*James 4:7 Submit yourselves therefore to God. Resist the devil, and he will flee from you*). Before demons and filth will leave you, you have to fall out of agreement with it. The devil and his filth cannot stay if there is nothing in you wanting him to remain. You have to break every covenant with it, divorce it, and resist it from being a part of your life. Spend time breaking covenants with the devil, sin, pleasures of sin, mindsets, errors, and anything that keeps you in covenant with the enemy and his filthiness.

- **Breaking Soul ties** – Soul ties can be Godly or ungodly in nature. And just how generational curses are passed down soul ties are transferred from you and the other person and vice versa. Soul ties can be formed through close friendships and interactions, covenants, vows, commitments, promises, physical intimacy. You can also have a soul tie by having an unhealthy attachment to something or someone that has taken the place of God in your life or that has become an addiction in your life. Your soul, heart, mind, and body can be intertwined, bound, knitted, or in covenant with that person, place or thing. You also exchange parts of yourself with the person you are in a soul tie with. Parts of their personality, soul, heart, thoughts, mindsets, character, nature, and other deposits, infuse you and begin to influence and live in you. Also, whomever they have had relationship with and have not cleansed themselves of, is being passed on to you and vice versa.

Godly Soul tie - 1Samuel 18:1 *And it came to pass, when he had made an end of speaking unto Saul, that the soul of Jonathan was knit with the soul of David, and Jonathan loved him as his own soul.*

> ***Ecclesiastes 4:9-12 The Amplified Bible***
> *Two are better than one, because they have a good [more satisfying] reward for their labor; For if they fall, the one will lift up his fellow. But woe to him who is alone when he falls and has not another to lift him up! Again, if two lie down together, then they have warmth; but how can one be warm alone? And though a man might prevail against him who is alone, two will withstand him. A threefold cord is not quickly broken.*

Matthew 18:19 Again I say unto you, That if two of you shall agree on earth as touching any thing that they shall ask, it shall be done for them of my Father which is in heaven.

Marriage Soul tie - *For this cause shall a man leave his father and mother, and shall be joined unto his wife, and they two shall be one flesh.*

Ungodly Soul tie - *Corinthians 6:16 What? know ye not that he which is joined to an harlot is one body? for two, saith he, shall be one flesh.*

> *Genesis 34:1-3 And Dinah the daughter of Leah, which she bare unto Jacob went out to seethe daughters of the land. And when Shechem the son of Hamor the Hivite, prince of the country, saw her, he took her, and lay with her, and defiled her. And his soul clave unto Dinah the daughter of Jacob, and he loved the damsel, and spake kindly unto the damsel. Verse 8 And Hamor communed with them, saying the soul of my son Shechem longeth for your daughter: I pray you give her him to wife. Sexual involvement can form such entangling tentacles of soul ties that it is extremely hard to break off the relationship.*
>
> *Proverbs 5:20-24 And why wilt thou, my son, be ravished with a strange woman, and embrace the bosom of a stranger? For the ways of man are before the eyes of the Lord, and he pondereth all his goings. His own*

iniquities shall take the wicked himself, and he shall be holden with the cords of his sins. He shall die without instruction; and in the greatness of his folly he shall go astray.

Psalms 1:1 *Blessed is the man that walketh not in the counsel of the ungodly, nor standeth in the way of sinners, nor sitteth in the seat of the scornful*

2Corinthians 6:14-18 *Be ye not unequally yoked together with unbelievers: for what fellowship hath righteousness with unrighteousness? and what communion hath light with darkness? And what concord hath Christ with Belial? or what part hath he that believeth with an infidel? And what agreement hath the temple of God with idols? for ye are the temple of the living God; as God hath said, I will dwell in them, and walk in them; and I will be their God, and they shall be my people. Wherefore come out from among them, and be ye separate, saith the Lord, and touch not the unclean thing; and I will receive you, And will be a Father unto you, and ye shall be my sons and daughters, saith the Lord Almighty.*

Soul tie with a Place – Lot's wife had a soul tie with Sodom and Gomorrah. God was destroying the city because of the perversion, lewdness, and lawlessness. God only allowed so many to live and allowed them time to get out of the city before he *destroyed it. As they were walking out, Lot's wife looked back and turned into a pillar of salt.*

> ***Genesis 19:23-26*** *Then the Lord rained upon Sodom and upon Gomorrah brimstone and fire from the Lord out of heaven; And he overthrew those cities, and all the plain, and all the inhabitants of the cities, and that which grew upon the ground. But his wife looked back from behind him, and she became a pillar of salt.*

Even though God had graced her with deliverance, her eyes and heart had regard for what she was leaving behind and because her soul was still knitted to Sodom and Gomorrah, God caused her to perish with it.

Agreement with God's will for the relationship along with healthiness is important in a Godly Soul tie.

> ***Amos 3:3*** *Can two walk together, except they be agreed?*
>
> ***The Message Bible*** *Do two people walk hand in hand if they aren't going to the same place?*

When the agreement is unhealthy, it causes for an ungodly soul tie. Also regardless to whether you agree or not, if a soul tie is formed, it has to be broken in order for you to be free of whatever was knitted and transferred through that tie. This is vital as rape, incest, abuse, mind control, religious sects, erred beliefs, etc. are ties that form without our agreement, out of ignorance, fear, or lack of knowledge, depending on the circumstance. But because they are not broken, whatever the offender deposited lives in us. Some people result in manifesting traits of their offender, while others live in the false identity of what was deposited. It is important to break and cleanse soul ties. This can be done by

- Spending time before the Lord identifying every ungodly soul tie you have.
- Confessing and repenting for your role in the soul tie, even if it was just giving into the lies and false identity of your offender.
- Forgiving the person you had a soul tie with and forgiving yourself for engaging in the soul tie.
- Breaking and removing the soul tie. Be sure to call out every person's name you have a soul tie with, go through these steps, and break and remove each tie.
- Using the blood of Jesus and the fire of God, cleanse yourself of all ungodly deposits and command any parts of your soul, heart, mind and identity to be restored back to you.

- Occasionally spend time, cleansing out any unhealthiest in your Godly soul tie relationships and any deposits that may have come from misunderstanding, miscommunication, taking one another for granted, being more to one another than God was saying, or becoming lax, fleshy or imbalanced in your interactions.

SPIRITS THAT ATTACK DANCE MINISTERS & DANCE MINISTRIES

Sometimes the power of dance ministers and dance ministries are overlooked, especially when it comes to dismantling, disempowering, displacing, and annihilating demonic forces. What tends to be even more overlooked is how demonic forces attack and oppress dance ministers and dance ministries. The only difference between dance ministers and ministers is dancers get about ten minutes to deliver their word and ministers get about 30 minutes to an hour to deliver their word. Dance ministers have the benefit of being able to visualize their word through movement, while using their movement to establish God's word in the people, the ground, the atmosphere and the region.

Demonic forces know the power of dance, this is the reason, the world is flooded with music, song, and movement that draws people to the demonic realm where idolatry, witchcraft, perversion and inordinacy can rule people's lives, platforms, and regions.

God created dance. Not the devil. In Genesis 1, God's spirit moved about as he created the heavens and the earth. *Moved* is *rahap* in the Hebrew and means *"to brood, flutter, to shake, to grow, to relax over."* These are all dance words. When we are going forth in dance ministry, we are ministering inside the presence of God, and his presence in us is moving within that atmosphere to create (reveal and grow) the word and will of God. This means that dancers are automatically considered "imparters" It is important to strive to live as a clean vessel because whatever is in a dancer, has the potential to be imparted into people, the land, atmosphere and region as we go forth in ministry.

> ***Genesis 1:1-2*** *In the beginning God created the heaven and the earth. And the earth was without form, and void; and darkness was upon the face of the deep. And the Spirit of God moved upon the face of the waters.*

Dancers and entertainers of the world know they are imparters. This is the reason they conjure up demonic spirits and allow them to possess their lives. They know that as they conjure up spirits, the spirits in them will impart things into people to draw them to further listening to their songs, watching their videos and tv shows, and attending their concerts. WHEWWW! We must know the power of impartation within us as dance ministers so we can birth forth miracles, signs and wonders when we minister.

Since the devil knows that dance ministers are "imparters" he strives to keep us bound with his evil spirits or he is constantly attacking us so we can be distracted and cannot adequately discern what God is speaking or doing, or what is needed in a ministry piece such that we will be effective against his workings. He also wants to keep us focused on just being praise and worshippers, rather than effective dance ministers who understand our power and authority and be void of revelation of what we are doing when we go forth in ministry. Without vision, the people (the dance minister) perishes (Proverbs 29:18). So basically because many dance ministers lack vision of the full purpose of our ministry:

- Religion annihilates us by speaking evil against our ministry so it is not welcomed in churches, ministries and regions.
- Tradition annihilates us by saying we have no purpose in churches, ministries, and regions.
- The world annihilates us by using their perversion and even training to make us look like we spew unholiness in the church or we are not technically or educationally equipped to minister.
- The devil annihilates us by wreaking warfare in our lives, homes, practices, ministries, and ministry engagements, because he recognizes when a dance minister goes forth, things are being spiritually birthed, developed, and released, and he is not trying to have that occur in his midst.
- We annihilate ourselves by not being delivered from shyness, insecurity, unworthiness, rejection, rebellion, lust, seduction, perversion, offense, pride, thus when we minister in dance, these strongholds and identity issues manifest in our movement.
- We annihilate ourselves by not recognizing that when our body moves, it stirs a war.

Whether we like it or not, our movement is starting a fight. We are striking and trampling, towering over, pushing back, tearing down, pushing out, dethroning, and overthrowing the kingdom of darkness.

We see this in *Genesis 1:1-2* as God's spirit moved to make the earth, His spirit annihilated darkness and the voids that were present, while bringing light and creation into fusion.

Since we are starting a fight when we dance, it is important to be offensive in knowing who and what we are combating so we can be effective ministers of movement.

Offensive Versus Defensive
Definition of Offensive:
1. making attack, aggressive, of relating to, or designed for attack
2. to be irritating or annoying, angering
3. giving painful or unpleasant sensations : nauseous, obnoxious, causing displeasure or resentment, disrespectful, insulting; displeasing
4. the position or attitude of aggression or attack
5. an aggressive movement or attack
6. attempting to score or one up your opponent
7. **Synonyms**: abhorrent, abusive, annoying, biting, cutting, detestable, disagreeable, discourteous, distasteful, dreadful,

embarrassing, evil, foul, ghastly, grisly, gross, hideous, horrible, horrid, impertinent, insolent, invidious, irritating, nauseating, objectionable, obnoxious, odious, off-color, offending, opprobrious, outrageous, repellent, reprehensible, repugnant, repulsive, revolting, rotten, rude, shocking, stinking, terrible, uncivil, unmannerly

On the defense you are trying to stop an opponent from their attack. On the offense you are striving to attack your opponent while gaining leverage or victory before being attacked.

We SHIFT from just thinking we are praisers and worshippers! We are WARRIORS! Our praise and worship and ministry of dance in general, annihilate the enemies of God, while ushering in his kingdom. #SHIFT

DEMONIC SPIRITS THAT ATTACK THE IDENTITY OF DANCE MINISTERS

When we are ministering a choreographed piece, it can be for the audience, the atmosphere, the region and/or unto the Lord. However, in order for people to connect to what we are ministering, we must involve them. It is essential to know when to engage the audience and when to be an expression and demonstration of the ministry we are doing. Balance in these areas is key to delivering and imparting God's message effectively where deliverance, healing and miracles follow.

One of the most challenging things to watch is someone ministering before you with their head up in the air, or looking down at the floor or even past you, like they are ignoring you. What is actually manifesting are identity issues that have intertwined themselves in their personality. Thus when we minister they are displayed in our movement.

Identity is the specific unique design and make up of a person, including the attributes and nature of who a person was created to be and who God is in that person. When there is brokenness or challenges in our identity, they manifest as shyness, fear, condemnation in the form of guilt and shame, insecurity/low self-esteem, rejection, pride, etc.

Because of this, the audience tends to be more focused on the reason the dancer got up to minister in the first place rather than the message. The audience is striving to find sympathy or empathy for the issues the dancer is exuding more so than the ministry that is going forth. When the audience claps, it is generally to encourage the dancer when the whole point of that person ministering was to empower and transform them.

We cannot wait until we get before the people to get delivered from identity issues. First of all people will fail you as they tend to applaud and respond to us based on whether we impacted them. If we are expecting them to validate us, we end up operating in impure motives that is more about getting our needs for approval met, than delivering the message and will of God.

Moreover, **1Corinthians 1:29** contends 'that no flesh should glory in his presence."

Flesh can entail sin issues, but is also anything that is carnal or not in the nature or character of God.

In this particular scripture the word *glory* means to "*boast or become vain*" and the word *presence* means "*to be in the face of or to come into sight.*"

So what happens is, if we are **NOT** dealing with our identity issues of shyness, insecurity, fear, etc., in our personal prayer time, when we begin to minister and illuminate the presence of God, the light of the glory gives sight to these issues.

And even if we are not a boastful person, these issues are exposed as they attempt to compete with the presence of God that is illuminating before us. They therefore become known to the people and before God. And though people may be blessed by our dance, they are not transformed because of the mixture that our issues are manifesting in the glory of God.

Let's explore some of these identity issues and what they are speaking about us when they are glorying (boasting) in the presence of God:

- **Shyness** is a form of fear that manifests as being bashful, easily frightened away; timid, suspicious; distrustful, reluctant; guarded, deficient, not bearing or breeding freely (producing or reproducing freely). Though it is natural to be nervous as this shows our dependence of God, we should not be shy or fearful. The scriptures lets us know that fear, shyness, timidity, etc., is a demonic spirit. **2Timothy 1:7** states *"For God hath not given us the spirit of fear (timidity, fearfulness, cowardice); but of power, and of love, and of a sound mind."*

    Shyness can be crippling and yields that the person feels that they will not be accepted, will not be understood, and/or has a fear of failing. Shyness tends to be a self-centered state, as the person is really revealing that in their hearts they are desperately seeking approval from others; but when around or before people, they strive to hide within themselves, hide in the floor by starring at the ground, or hide in the presence by staring in sky, hide off in space by staring past the people, for fear of not receiving the approval they so desperately desire.

- **Fear** is a distressing emotion, concern or anxiety aroused by impending danger, evil, pain, sweating, rejection, etc., whether the threat is real or imagined; it is the feeling or condition of being afraid. When fear boasts in the presence of God it displays our thoughts of not feeling capable, equipped, valued, secure, trusted, disciplined, controlled and whole. It is basically displaying that there is something in our personality and character that requires deliverance and healing. When fear manifests in the dance, it appears as anxiety, panic; we may exhibit wide eyes and as if we are frightened and just want to run from before the people. Our movements may appear disheveled or frenzied and maybe quick as if we are just striving to get the ministry piece over with. Fear can also manifest with such a grip that the person will be ministering the dance, but the movement will be stiff and barely presentable as fear will be wrapped around the person or has a hold of the person's heart and soul, where they are restricted in their movement.

- **Condemnation** means to give judgment against, to judge worthy of punishment and/or to feel and operate as if others have judged even though a sentence may not have been passed yet. Condemnation causes us to operate in guilt and shame.

   Guilt insinuates that we have committed or feel responsible for an offense, crime, violation, or wrong.

   Shame is a painful feeling arising from the consciousness of something dishonorable, improper, ridiculous, etc., done by oneself or another. It is also a feeling disgrace or regret.

   When we minister with issues of shame and guilt, we attempt to become faceless before the people. So in essence, when we come before the people to minister if there are unhealed or unrepented areas of condemnation that are not dealt with, we enter in a disposition of shame and guilt where pain, over emotionalism or even little to no emotion or movement is displayed.

   For example, a person can be bound to the point where he or she hides within themselves and no emotion is displayed in their facial expression or in their body movement when they are ministering. It is almost as if the person is lethargic and motionless as they fear being judged or they have already judged themselves so they are not free in the expression of their dance.

And often the person who experiences condemnation can only express emotion when the ministry is about pain or hurt and even in these instances, the ministry is more erratic and overly emotional than expressing balanced emotion and movement that displays the heart of the message of God. The ministry the person is exuding is often in attempt to compensate and pay the debt for judgment that has them bound. The ministry piece in turn becomes more about the person ministering than the people, atmosphere or region they are to be ministering to.

- **Inadequacy, Insecurity, & Low Self-Esteem**
I would define inadequacy as, *"having a feeling of deficiency, feeling incomplete or insufficient regarding life or for a position, task or duty."*

    Dictionary.com defines *inadequate* as:
    1. not adequate or sufficient; inept or unsuitable
    2. psychiatry: ineffectual in response to emotional, social, intellectual, and physical demands in the absence of any obvious mental or physical deficiency

    In collaboration with Dictionary.com, I would define *insecurity* as, *"a lack of confidence or assurance; self-doubt, instability, inferiority, low self-esteem, fear of what others will think, timidity, shyness, embarrassment, self-consciousness, uncertainty."*

I would define *low self-esteem* as *"having a general negative overall opinion of oneself, judging or evaluating oneself negatively, and placing a general negative value on oneself as a person."*

A dancer who is insecure, inadequate or of low self-esteem will attempt to hide within themselves or behind others when they minister in dance. They often do not dance with their entire bodies as movements are restricted and close to the body, and they have minimal to no ability to interpret movement through their personality or character.
- Their movements may look like everyone else's but lack personality.
- Their movements may mimic others who they want to be like.
- Their movements may also be bland and ineffective due to having no personal identity and character regarding who they are in God and his purpose and call upon their lives.

- **<u>Rejection</u>** means to throw away, as anything useless or vile, to cast off; to forsake, to refuse to receive; to slight; to despise.

  Because a person is dealing with issues of rejection, they are already in a place of separation before they even begin minister. They have already ostracized and separated themselves from the audience. This is because they lack the ability to connect or fear connecting, so they self-reject to protect themselves from being rejected.

Therefore the rejected person attempts to get their needs met for approval and belonging through their giftings and calling. Their ministry of dance manifests as pride or superiority, for the person presents as having a high or inordinate opinion of themselves. Yet they really are not prideful or haughty. Truthfully they are insecure, but are masking it with a false confidence of self.

This person will dance to be seen. Their dancing will be attention seeking, overly dramatic and distracting, such that they receive the approval and accolades for their gifting and ministry. It will be about them and not about God and his message or work in the people, atmosphere, and/or region.

- o Sidebar comment: A person who has unresolved issues of abuse, tends to manifests the spirit of the offender or the victim when ministering.

- **Pride** means a high or inordinate opinion of one's own dignity, importance, merit, or superiority, whether as cherished in the mind or as displayed in capabilities, character, conduct, etc.

  The prideful dancer will present as if they are coming to transform the audience and get them right in the eyes of God. They will not exude any humility where they are a testimony of what they are ministering, such that they have worked to the word or message in their own lives. The prideful dancer minister dances alone and their movements and expressions are more of one who dictates and orders others around. There is no sense of team or ministry with others, as it is all about "me, myself and I," while stealing God's glory.

- **Lust** manifests in the dance it can be very sensual, wooing, sexy and physically and emotionally seductive. One of the challenges with lust is that it causes others to stumble. It is a spirit that tempts or entices by tapping into the vulnerable and unhealed areas of a person's challenges, and plants inordinate seeds and thoughts to trigger blatant sin. Lust tends to mesmerize the souls, hearts, emotions and flesh of people rather than pierce the spirit where people can be transformed.

    Matthew 5:28 But I say unto you, That whosoever looketh on a woman to lust after her hath committed adultery with her already in his heart. And if thy right eye offend thee, pluck it out, and cast it from thee: for it is profitable for thee that one of thy members should perish, and not that thy whole body should be cast into hell.

    The Amplified Version *But I say to you that everyone who so much as looks at a woman with evil desire for her has already committed adultery with her in his heart. If your right eye serves as a trap to ensnare you or is an occasion* *for you to stumble and sin, pluck it out and throw it away. It is better that you lose one of your members than that your whole body be cast into hell (Gehenna).*

Lust means *"to desire to have a thing or to covet."* It means *"to desire wrongfully, inordinately, or without due regard for the rights of others."*

Dictionary.com defines *lust* as:
1. intense sexual desire or appetite
2. uncontrolled or illicit sexual desire or appetite; lecherousness
3. a passionate or overmastering desire or craving

We are quick to say "*I was just looking or I was just thinking but I did not touch*" however, Jesus warns us that the operation of lust is so subtle that even looking at a woman and desiring or thinking of her past a place of admiration is a sin. Because we are constantly being tempted by the world, media, and the enemy in effort to draw us into things that are not beneficial to us, or to gluten for, or illegally obtain more of what is beneficial to us (e.g. Food, clothes, sex, idolatry), as ministers we should always be cleansing out lust even if we are not in blatant sin. We could be housing lust and not even know it, or be so comfortable with lusting and being enticed to things in a covetous nature that we are desensitized to the presence of lust within us.

Though we cannot control how a person lusts after us, we can control what is in us so that when people watch us minister, all they see is the virtuous power of God. If there is any lust in us when we go forth and minister, and even while we are preparing for ministry, it will manifest. It will manifest in our hips, in our eyes, in the sensuality and presentation of our movement, etc. Lust also manifests as spooky spiritual or bewitching. It has a texture, presentation and movement that draws a person to it rather than to the entire ministry, or to the spirit of God. It then provokes lustful thoughts that draws a person into sin if they do not cast them down **(2Corinthians 10:5)**

I want to encourage dancers to be careful of lust even after they minister. Sometimes people will want to converse about your ministry after the service and even want to shake your hand and/or hug you. There is nothing wrong with this, however, we must be careful of lust spirits that can transfer from those who are drawn to your ministry. Some may not even be aware of what they need deliverance from, but because we use our bodies to minister, we should be keen in being able to detect when something has come upon us or in us that is not like the Holy Spirit.

***1Corinthians 6:18-19** What? know ye not that your body is the temple of the Holy Ghost which is in you, which ye have of God, and ye are not your own? For ye* *are bought with a price: therefore glorify God in your body, and in your spirit, which are God's.*

<u>Glorify</u> in the Greek is *doxazō* and means:
1. to render (or esteem) glorious (in a wide application): — (make) glorify(-ious), full of (have) glory, honor
2. to think, suppose, be of opinion, to praise, extol, magnify, celebrate to honor, do honor to, hold in honor, to make glorious
3. adorn with lustre, clothe with splendor, to impart glory to something, render it excellent to make renowned, render illustrious
4. to cause the dignity and worth of some person or thing to become manifest and acknowledged

We glorify God in our bodies by seeking to be pure vessels where he can fully dwell. Some ways I keep my body pure is that I spend time washing and purging my body, soul, mind, emotions, appetite, and thought life, in the blood of Jesus, then I soak myself in the virtue, purity, righteousness, holiness and glory of God. There are also times where I will use the holy fire of God to burn out ungodly roots, demonic impartations and imprints, demonic, soulish or emotional fruits, warfare darts and words coming from people and the enemy. I do this:

- After I minister as I cleanse myself of anything that may have transferred from

- the atmosphere, region, and/or people that I ministered too
- After work or after I have been around people where carnality, compromise or sin dwelled, or when being in a situation that has been trying, perverted, lustful, full of witchcraft or idolatry etc. Because the world is so infiltrated such places could be as simple as going to the mall, out to dinner with friends or family, visiting family and friends, etc.
- At times when I have watched things on TV that are full of lust, sin, perversion, idolatry, blood and gore. I try to avoid media with these things in it but even commercials, kid shows, rated PG shows entail these negative attributes
- After scrolling on social media, as many videos, pictures, articles are full of mess and so I cleanse myself to keep myself holy as possible unto the Lord

The more you cleanse yourself, the keener you will be in discerning what is not like the Holy Spirit and the more God's power and authority can live and work through you for his glory.

SPIRITS THAT ATTACK PRACTICES & MINISTRY ENGAGEMENTS

The Lord has revealed these spirits to me over the years while preparing for different events. We experienced a lot of warfare and was able to discern what spirits were attacking us personally, the atmosphere and the ministry we were striving to birth forth.

Deaf and Dumb Spirit - inability or challenge to hear God regarding movement or choreography, or to see movement in one's spiritual imagination. Many times this can be characterized by an inability to connect to what you hear being spoken or revealed to you by God, and what you see being taught. You will hear God regarding what the movement should look like, or what He is saying for an engagement but there will be disconnect in your ability to actually comprehend, understand it, and then produce movement in accordance to it. Dance leaders will teach the members movement, and share with them what they are hearing, but despite speaking and teaching the movement, there will be a disconnect in their ability to truly comprehend and grasp the movement in their spiritual imagination, which will hinder their natural body from reproducing it.

A person being attacked by the deaf and dumb spirit:

- Will at times have a confused, and puzzled look on their face. They may also look as though they are not there and are spaced out
- Will become easily frustrated with themselves because they can hear what you are saying and see what you are doing, but they cannot understand it, and cannot get their body to reproduce the movement
- Will need things repeated and showed to them over and over, and will be very forgetful
- When you ask them questions they will be confused and unable to answer effectively
- They will do the movement with you, but when you ask them to do it alone they will not be able to because no true comprehension or understanding took place as you were teaching
- You will have insight from God but you will not be able to write it down, speak it, or truly understand it
- You will have the feeling of "awe man it is right there" but have no ability to grasp it

Isaiah 6:9 And he said, Go, and tell this people, Hear ye indeed, but understand not; and see ye indeed, but perceive not.

Mark 4:12 That seeing they may see, and not perceive; and hearing they may hear, and not understand; lest at any time they should be converted, and their sins should be forgiven them.

Zapping Spirit - steals movement and choreography by jolting them out of the memory of the brain such that the brain cannot send the correct signals to the body.

<u>*Zap* in Dictionary.com means:</u>
1. to kill or shoot.
2. to attack, defeat, or destroy with sudden speed and force.
3. to bombard with electrical current, radiation, laser beams, etc.
4. to strike or jolt suddenly and forcefully.
5. to cook in a microwave oven.
6. to skip over or delete (TV commercials), as by switching channels or pushing a fast-forward button on a playback device:

When a zapping spirit is at work it is literally killing, shooting, and deleting movement, revelation, and understanding from your mind, and it is happening with a sudden speed and force. This is why you can be executing the movements in one moment, but within the next moment you can no longer remember it or can execute it. There is a striking and jolting that is occurring spiritually, and you are being bombarded with demonic electrical currents, radiation, and laser beams that are causing death to your ability to retain movement, revelation, and vision.

John 10:10 The thief cometh not, but for to steal, and to kill, and to destroy: I am come that they might have life, and that they might have it more abundantly.

Cloaking spirit – disguises movement and choreography where the leader and the dance ministers cannot spiritually see the appearance of it. The movement or choreography is masked where it looks like an illusion of its true form. The cloaking spirit will have members improvising their own movement based off of what they think it should be or what they thought was taught, rather than making sure they are ministering the correct movement and/or choreography. The leader will continue to have to correct the dancer, while letting them know that though they have an appearance or impression of the movement, it is not the correct movement that is being taught. As the leader there will also be times where you will be choreographing and you believe that you have the correct movement but you will continually feel as though you are missing something and that it is not the correct movement to be taught to your team. This could be an indication that the cloaking spirit is at work.

> *2Corinthians 11:13-14 For such are false apostles, deceitful workers, transforming themselves into the apostles of Christ. And no marvel; for Satan himself is transformed (disguised, transfigure) into an angel of light.*

The Deaf and Dumb, Zapping, Cloaking, and Blocking spirits, can operate through witchcraft spell attacks that are sent against ministries to steal and hide movement or cause the brain not to remember movement. When they come as spells, there can

sometimes be a mist or darkness in the atmosphere or around a person. The dancer(s) may also experience dizziness, blurriness, or pressure in and around the head.
When these spirits operate, bind and cast them out and sever every alliance to any spirits that may be operating in the atmosphere or territory.

- When the death and dumb spirit manifests command spiritual hearing and visualization to come to the ears and eyes and for the eyes of the understanding to be enlightened so that the dancer can perceive, retain and sustain in movement, choreography and revelation.
- Cleanse the zapping spirit out of the atmosphere and out of the dance ministers. Command movements, choreography, and revelation that has been zapped out to be restored.
- When the cloaking spirit manifests counterattack it by calling forth God's truth for the dance piece and an illumination of his will to radiate regarding the dance and choreography.

Romans 12:2 And be not conformed to this world: but be ye transformed by the renewing of your mind, that ye may prove what [is] that good, and acceptable, and perfect, will of God.

Philippians 4:8 - Finally, brethren, whatsoever things are true, whatsoever things [are] honest, whatsoever things [are] just, whatsoever things [are] pure, whatsoever things [are] lovely, whatsoever things [are] of good report; if [there be] any virtue, and if [there be] any praise, think on these things.

2Corinthians 10:3-5 *For though we walk in the flesh, we do not war after the flesh: (For the weapons of our warfare are not carnal, but mighty through God to the pulling down of strong holds;) Casting down imaginations, and every high thing that exalteth itself against the knowledge of God, and bringing into captivity every thought to the obedience of Christ*

James 4:7 *Submit yourselves therefore to God. Resist the devil, and he will flee from you.*

Isaiah 26:3 - *Thou wilt keep [him] in perfect peace, [whose] mind [is] stayed [on thee]: because he trusteth in thee.*

Blocking Spirits - blocking spirits use walls, barriers or troops of demons that have locked themselves together in the spirit realm, where a dance minister or dance team will have difficulty getting pass a particular part of a dance piece. Dance ministers keep making mistakes, cannot see the ministry piece past that a particular movement; or the dancer keeps ministering the piece to a particular part of the dance, but cannot bypass it.

Psalms 18:29 *For by thee I have run through a troop; and by my God have I leaped over a wall.*

This scriptures lets us know that we must run through these barriers. So when encountering them in your practices or life in general, verbally declare out blasting through any troops that have set up siege against you and then use your authority in God to leap over demonic structures.

Python Spirits - wrap around a person's mind or body to squeeze and restrict them where:

- They are limited in their movement
- There may also be an unexplainable tiredness and lethargic oppression where the person finds it difficult to move.
- They feel so weighty, they are physically suffocating, overly exerted in energy, and they are not able to physically keep up with the momentum of the dance
- It causes confusion, discombobulation, double mindedness, and thought racing, from the signal faculties in the brain being restricted, weighty, and crushed

Isaiah 61:3 To appoint unto them that mourn in Zion, to give unto them beauty for ashes, the oil of joy for mourning, the garment of praise for the spirit of heaviness; that they might be called trees of righteousness, the planting of the Lord, that he might be glorified.

Loose Holy fire to torment it where it releases its grip, while commanding this spirit to uncoil and be cast out of your midst.

Spirit of Leviathan - interrupts and distorts communication between the speaker and the listener. Its' effort is to sow offense, discord, misunderstanding, faultfinding, ungodly judging, mistrust and suspicion. Someone will say one thing and the person will misinterpret it. A matter that is mediocre can be taken out of proportion where drama and discord arise. Dance ministers are offended and not even sure why. Their offense will change the atmosphere of the practice, allowing irritation and tempers to flare quickly. Job speaks of how Leviathan operates in *Job 41:26-32*. This spirit was at operation between him and his friends who were striving to understand why God allowed the enemy to bring havoc upon his life. This spirit also distorted Job's views where he could not receive wise counsel from God during this time of trial with the Lord. This spirit will enter in when the ministry is under heavy warfare, is in the middle of intense ministry or transition, or is on a time schedule with completing a ministry piece.

The quickest way to rid a dancer, the ministry, and the atmosphere of this spirit is to repent quickly of any irritation, drama and discord; forgive and reunite in heart and spirit one to another. The unity and love of Christ will dismantle and displace this spirit.

Galatians 6:1-3 The Amplified Bible
BRETHREN, IF any person is overtaken in misconduct or sin of any sort, you who are spiritual [who are responsive to and controlled by the Spirit] should set him right and restore and reinstate him, without any sense of superiority and with all gentleness, keeping an attentive eye on yourself, lest you should be tempted also. Bear (endure, carry) one another's burdens and troublesome moral faults, and in this way fulfill and observe perfectly the law of Christ (the Messiah) and complete what is lacking [in your obedience to it].

Mind Binding & Mind Blinding Spirits – operate through the stronghold of mind control. These spirits bind and blind the thought life, the mind and senses to cause affliction, confusion, unexplainable fear of people or of failure, and anxiety. This spirit tends to operate and look like an octopus or a squid. You may feel pressure or a tormenting headache, feel like something is sticking you in the eyes, ears, temples, forehead, or the back of the head. Things may look black as you strain to see and discern spiritually and naturally. You may become dull of hearing because the ears will feel clogged or like something is lodged in them. It may also feel like something is sitting on your head or wrapped around your head.

This stronghold of mind control may also plague you with vile, perverse, unnecessary, or unimportant thoughts. Or may have you panicking and thinking of something over and over to distract you from what is presently important. Sometimes this spirit will swamp you with constant thoughts of hurts from your past or present life and heart issues that are unresolved. You may find it difficult to pay attention or to press forward in working on present tasks because of these constant plaguing thoughts and feelings of intense pressure.

> ***Proverbs 15:15 The Amplified Bible*** *All the days of the desponding and afflicted are made evil [by anxious thoughts and forebodings (prophecy)], but he who has a glad heart has a continual feast [regardless of circumstances].*

Ask the Lord to sever the tentacles of this spirit or use the sword of the spirit to cut them. Break the power of pressure, pain and torment, and release healing where needed.

Spirit of Void and Darkness - may be at work when there are no blockages, hinderances, blinding, binding, confusion or discombobulation, yet the atmosphere, eye gates, imagination and mind is totally black and blank, dark and empty.

We see this spirit in operation in ***Genesis 1:2*** when God was creating the heavens and the earth.

> *And the earth was without form, and void; and darkness was upon the face of the deep. And the Spirit of God moved upon the face of the waters*

This spirit wants you to think that everything is dead and without form, you cannot see or discern properly, or that there is no potential for creation or manifestation. It operates like a black blanket or cloud, covering everything so you cannot see behind the scenes. It will smother blackness and void over the plans and seeds of God, and even conceal demonic plans so you cannot be offensive against the enemy.

It will black out the ability to form and create movement and choreography, while covering up revelation, purpose for ministry engagements, and plots and plans of the enemy.

> **Daniel 2:22** *He reveals the deep and secret things; He knows what is in the darkness, and the light dwells with Him.*

When this spirit attacks begin to release and declare the light, wisdom, and profound, searchable, secretive, mysteries of God to come forth to dispel the darkness. Also, as a dancer you possess the word and illuminating presence of God therefore, you can combat this spirit with your dance to fill the void and fill the darkness.

The Deaf & Dumb, Zapping, Cloaking, Blocking, Python, Leviathan, Mind Binder & Mind Blinder & Void Spirits:
- Prolong the ability to see the ministry assignment clearly
- Prevents and hinders your ability to see into the region, church, ministry, or etc that you are preparing to minister too

- Prolong leaders ability to receive movement and choreography from the Holy Spirit
- Prolong and hinder the progress of practices and cause the necessity for additional practices
- Prolong or hinder members' and ministries' ability to learn movement and choreography
- Cause frustration, division, and distractions against and within the ministry due to having to constantly teach and review movement and choreography

Dance ministers are open doors for these spirits:
- When they do not practice on their own and tend to only practice when the team practices
- When there is no personal cultivation of their gifting
- When they are stressed, and tired
- Have challenges balancing their home, school, work, and ministry life
- Have a need for attention and use practice as a way to receive attention from the leader or members
- Operating in the spirit of inadequacy, insecurity, rejection, the little girl or little boy spirit
- And this also can just operate as a demonic attack to hinder the ministry from going forth

We must adhere to the word of God so we can equip ourselves against these spirits.

When you fortify yourself in the truth of these scriptures it is difficult for these spirits to gain entrance into your life and ministry:

> **Romans 12:2** *And be not conformed to this world: but be ye transformed by the renewing of your mind, that ye may prove what [is] that good, and acceptable, and perfect, will of God.*
>
> **Philippians 4:8** - *Finally, brethren, whatsoever things are true, whatsoever things [are] honest, whatsoever things [are] just, whatsoever things [are] pure, whatsoever things [are] lovely, whatsoever things [are] of good report; if [there be] any virtue, and if [there be] any praise, think on these things.*
>
> **2Corinthians 10:3-5** *For though we walk in the flesh, we do not war after the flesh: (For the weapons of our warfare are not carnal, but mighty through God to the pulling down of strong holds;) Casting down imaginations, and every high thing that exalteth itself against the knowledge of God, and bringing into captivity every thought to the obedience of Christ*
>
> **James 4:7** *Submit yourselves therefore to God. Resist the devil, and he will flee from you.*

> *Isaiah 26:3* - *Thou wilt keep [him] in perfect peace, [whose] mind [is] stayed [on thee]: because he trusteth in thee.*

These are some strategies to fortify yourself and team against these spirits:
- Praying before practices and engagements against zapping, cloaking, blocking, witchcraft, Python, mind binding, mind blinding spirits
- Cleanse out stress, tiredness, weariness, etc.
- Close up open doorways in the team and spirit realm that would cause these spirits to operate.
- As they manifest during practices and engagements, take a moment to use the prayer strategies that were discussed and other revelation that God gives you to cast them out of your midst.

Little Girl or Little Boy Spirit - This is a spirit where a person has had a traumatic or painful experience in their childhood and parts of their personality are stuck at that age or are stuck in that stressful, or traumatic event. Because they need deliverance and healing from this experience, they tend to fluctuate between their current age and the age of the traumatic event. A person with a little girl/boy spirit could have experienced a lack of development in an age or stage of life and thus the spirit of the little girl or little boy manifest in them. This person will throw tantrums, sulk, be drama focused, always need prayer for something, can be very passive aggressive and defiant when he or she does not get their way and will do things for attention. They will constantly ask questions and desire help with movement and choreography that they have the ability to grasp. But due to the need for attention, love and constant reassurance, they will drain the leader, members and atmosphere of the ministry through the manifestation of this demonic spirit.

Sometimes dance ministers with this spirit will quit the ministry over small matters that could be resolved with communication. They may also display a pattern of quitting then returning as the little girl and little boy in them has a challenge committing to the adult responsibilities of ministry.

> *1Corinthians 24:20* Brethren, be not children in understanding: howbeit in malice be ye children, but in understanding be men.
>
> *1Corinthians 13:11* When I was a child, I spake as a child, I understood as a child, I thought as a child: but when I became a man, I put away childish things.
>
> *1Corinthians 4:14-15* That we henceforth be no more children, tossed to and fro, and carried about with every wind of doctrine, by the sleight of men, and cunning craftiness, whereby they lie in wait to deceive; But speaking the truth in love, may grow up into him in all things, which is the head, even Christ: From whom the whole body fitly joined together and compacted by that which every joint supplieth, according to the effectual working in the

measure of every part, maketh increase of the body unto the edifying of itself in love.

Inadequacy, Insecurity, & Low Self-Esteem
I would define inadequacy as, *"having a feeling of deficiency, feeling incomplete or insufficient regarding life or for a position, task or duty."*

Dictionary.com defines *inadequate* as:
1. not adequate or sufficient; inept or unsuitable
2. psychiatry: ineffectual in response to emotional, social, intellectual, and physical demands in the absence of any obvious mental or physical deficiency

In collaboration with Dictionary.com, I would define *insecurity* as, *"a lack of confidence or assurance; self-doubt, instability, inferiority, low self-esteem, fear of what others will think, timidity, shyness, embarrassment, self-consciousness, uncertainty."*

I would define *low self-esteem* as *"having a general negative overall opinion of oneself, judging or evaluating oneself negatively, and placing a general negative value on oneself as a person."*

When inadequacy, insecurity, and/or low self-esteem are in operation, a dance minister will desire to be used of God, but will require constant continual encouragement. This is because these spirits make people feel unworthy, and because they give into the perceptions of these spirits, they present and act as if they are unworthy. The person will sometimes feel and state that they cannot go forth due to some misperceived personality deficiency or misguided physical efficiency. They will want to change movements before even attempting to do them. And though they may be capable of doing a movement, some may contend the movement is difficult. The challenge is, the person is equipped but because they require constant encouragement, from people and from God, they can be draining to a dance leader and to those around them.

A person who is challenged by these demonic forces is often a risk to a dance ministry, because many of them tend to be unreliable, uncertain, and unstable in God. Many of them cannot be trusted with the mature things of God as they will lack follow through, then give unrealistic or untrue reasons for their actions. To them the reasons will appear valid, but to the ministry and to God, they will be invalid and irresponsible.

Spirit of the Outcast
Dictionary.com defines *outcast* as:
1. a person who is rejected or cast out, as from home or society
2. a homeless wanderer; vagabond
3. rejected, rejected matter, refused, discarded

My definition: Unwanted, dejected, rejected, belittled, devalued, and at times verbally ridiculed and abused

Ishmael and his maidservant mother was cast out of Abraham's home because Sarah did not want Ishmael to share the throne with Isaac *(Genesis 21:9-13)*.

The lepers in the bible were outcasts. They had to live alone and outside the camp of the Israelites *(Leviticus 13, Numbers 5:2)*.

David was often found outcast due to running from King Saul. King Saul was jealous of David's success. King Saul was often oppressed by a demonic spirit that David's playing of the harp would soothe him from. King Saul was challenged by being subjected to the very man that had the potential, favor, and positive qualities to rule his throne *(1 Samuel 18-22)*.

Many dance ministers have often felt like an outcast or have been outcast because of their ministry, or just being peculiar and not really fitting in, or being unable to define their anointing or mantle by general religious standards. Also, if a ministry happens to have a dance team, we find that some leaders will send the peculiar or rejected to the arts ministries when they do not know what to do with that person. So even though the person may not be a dance minister or supposed to be a part of the team, they are sometimes placed in these ministries because the "true" God ordained ministries of the church do not want to be bothered with them.

Sometimes the outcast dance minister is striving to escape religious and traditional perceptions manifesting through leaders or members who possess

the spirit of Saul. We learn about the spirit of Saul through the story of David *1Samuel 18-22*. A person with the Saul spirit
- fears change
- is insecure about ideas or new movements of God that is not their idea or that is unfamiliar
- or that they feel you pose a threat to their position or anointing

They may not have a revelation of dance ministry so they seek to ostracize or kill the dance minister and the dance team.

Within the scripture we find David, serving, honoring and running from Saul.

Psalms 105:15 David states, "Touch *not mine anointed, and do my prophets no harm."*

David was a warrior so in my opinion this scripture is saying that he was not going to physically harm Saul or intentionally harm Saul. He was not going to kill Saul or seek his life the way Saul did him. However, I do not believe it meant that David was to deny, hide, or not express the truth of what he was experiencing. David was being abused by Saul and there is no way to negate that.

Because we tend to make abused people feel disloyal or like sinners if they speak truth about what religious leaders and members have done to them, many outcast dance ministers suppress their hurts and pains. Many have been devalued, belittled, outcast, rejected, castaway, and exiled and as a result some have wandered from church to church, ministry to ministry, dance ministry to dance ministry, mentor to mentor like a lost vagabond or sick leper, striving to fit in and find someone who understands them or has a similar anointing as them. Many of these dance ministers are so wounded that by the time they find their fit, they are still unable to connect or feel safe, because they are bound in their experience as the outcast. It is as if the disease of the outcast is still on them despite now being in a ministry that accepts them and sees who they are.

The challenge with the spirit of the outcast, is that many in the body of Christ are starting to receive dance ministry and even desire it within their local assemblies and ministry services. However, some dance ministers still view themselves and display behaviors as outcasts. Most dance conferences, workshops and practices are centered around dance movement and the revelation of dance ministry, yet there is not many avenues for deliverance and healing regarding the persecution and ostracism, therefore many operate in a victim mentality.

Wikipedia.com define a victim mentality as *"an acquired (learned) personality trait in which a person tends to regard him or herself as a victim of the negative actions of others, and to think, speak and act as if that were the case – even in the absence of clear evidence. It depends on habitual thought processes and attribution."*

Some of the challenges and immaturity among dance ministries is not because we are not being received by Christendom, but because we are still operating in a victim mentality. We have to acquire deliverance and healing so we can adequately minister through our mantle with power, efficiency, and fruit/signs following.

Keys to Healing From the Spirit of the Outcast
- Spend time in prayer, acknowledge the abuse that occurred. Call it what it was and cancel all the confusion, excuses that others used and even you used to defend, protect, suppress, or remain in false obligation to those that abused you.
- Spend time in prayer forgiving those who ostracized and rejected you and release the situation for God to avenge.
- Cleanse all suppressed hurts and experiences out of your soul, heart and memories.
- Cast out spirits of the outcast, rejection, fear of rejection, self-rejection, vagabond, wandering, offense, defense, rage and anger, insecurity, inadequacy.
- Spend time soaking in the deliverance and healing power of God.

Outcast Youth
Christian dance teams for children and teenagers are often formed to give the youth something to do rather than really building with the mindset that dance is ministry. The children and teens are outcast because they are being grouped together and forced to

become the religious performance and entertainment for parents and loved ones to glory over during holidays and special occasions at church services. Most of the youth are being set apart from the general congregation, and are not taught true relationship with God, nor are they being cultivated in their anointing. Many youth dance ministries are designed to give the kiddos something to do so the adults can worship and do religious works. Thus further cultivating the mindset that dance is just performance and is not true ministry within the church.

This is a challenge to many dance ministers who have been religiously persecuted in effort to pioneer the ministry of dance into the body of Christ.

- Some have been told dance ministry is for kids and so no avenue has been provided for them to minister
- Some have been "patty caked" for their ministry as people do not embrace the deliverance and healing of the ministry
- Some have tried to change the mindset of the youth dance teams, but because it is just something to do, many leaders and parents:
    - Are not invested in bringing excellence to it
    - Do not want to purchase appropriate garments
    - Do not bring youth to practice consistently

- o Resist investing in conferences and workshops that teach the kids about the ministry of dance
- o Do not want to help youth practice at home or hold them accountable to practicing at home

Many parents and leaders view sports at school and in the community as more valuable than dance ministry or other ministries for youth within the church.

Dance ministers get caught in the middle of this mindset when they strive to bring correction to this misimpression, and when they themselves strive to go forth in their ministry. Therefore this is something that needs to be gutted out of the foundation of dance ministry as a whole, and new teaching foundation concerning dance ministry needs to be laid.

Those who are a part of the ministry need to be ones who are:

- Truly gifted in this area, not just anyone. If they are not gifted in this area and it is not a part of their calling and destiny, they will be out of alignment with God's destiny and plan for them, and they will never truly come into knowing who they really are and what their true gifts are because they were just outcast that have been placed into a ministry that is not a part of God's vision plan for them. This is

sad, because you have potential destiny dying within your ministry.
- Those who have a pure interest and pursuit in this area, even if their gift has not been fully unveiled or discovered yet.
- Those who are willing to do the work to cultivate their gifts, sow their time, finances, and etc, and those who can commit to being consistent in the ministry.

These things need to be taught as a standard of dance ministry teams, as with any other team like for example a basketball team, not just anyone can get up and play during the game. The players need to have the uniforms, the heart, passion, and talent for the game. They need to have been at practice consistently, and committed to getting better and better at their game. It is the same with dance ministry teams, they are not less than. And dance ministries have to stop settling for less, and stop allowing others to cause us to settle for less. As the dance minister it is important that we set the standard for our teams and that we do not allow others who do not have the vision for the ministry to set our standards. The pastor of the church may be able to support the vision, but he/she is not the visionary so they cannot be the ones who we allow to set the standards and the value of the ministry. It has to come through us, the visionary. We also have to stop setting our standards low out of a fear of losing people, and fear that people will not want to be a part, and that the standards are too high. (I can see some people not wanting to enforce these standards out of fear of people not wanting to be a part). If God gave you the standards for your team and they are aligned with the vision that he has given you, you have to trust God to bring the provision for the vision. He will bring the people who are called to be a part of the ministry, and who have the vision, the like spirit & like mindedness. These people will have the DNA of the ministry. Our focus cannot be on trying to fill the ministry with a whole bunch of people who truly are not called to dance ministry. We have to be ok with who God sends to be a part of the ministry because they will have its DNA and will have the ability to birth forth with you, and reproduce the DNA of the vision.

Controlling Spirits - The spirit of control will attempt to restrain, direct, curb the leader, members' movement, choreography, practice, and the vision of the dance to what he or she believes it should be. A person with this spirit is usually combative with leadership, resistant and closed to the leading of the Holy Spirit. This dance minister may at times, use sarcastic jokes, belittling or negative comments, and subtle remarks to sway members and the atmosphere of the practice or ministry to his or perception.

Sometimes this person may be jealous of the leader, and/or want to be the leader. Or they simply just have control issues, and difficulty submitting to anything that is not their idea or that is not under their power or jurisdiction.

> **Romans 16:17-18** *Now I beseech you, brethren, mark them which cause divisions and offences contrary to the doctrine which ye have learned; and avoid them. For they that are such serve not our Lord Jesus Christ, but their own belly; and by good words and fair speeches deceive the hearts of the simple.*

<u>Control</u> in Dictionary.com means:
1. to exercise restraint or direction over; dominate, command
2. to hold in check; curb
3. to test or verify (a scientific experiment) by a parallel experiment or other standard of comparison
4. to eliminate or prevent the flourishing or spread of

The agenda of a person operating in this spirit is:

- To try to dominate the group and the practice and take command over it, whether that be by constantly drawing attention to themselves or blatantly trying to make adjustments or changes to things
- To check and curb the team by always being the one to stop the progress and forward motion of the practice in means to have control over it

- To diminish and lessen the leader and team members
- To test the leader, the team members, the choreography, the revelation, and the instructions given to compare them to their standard of what is right
- To eliminate and prevent the flourishing of the gifts and callings of the entire team, and the spread and expansion of the vision of God for practices, engagements, leadership & authority, and the vision of the team in general

Spirits of Intimidation
Intimidation from Dictionary.com means:
1. to make timid; fill with fear.
2. to overawe or cow, as through the force of personality or by superior display of wealth, talent, etc.
3. to force into or deter from some action by inducing fear:

This spirit causes dance leaders and ministers to cower from who they are in God, and all that goes into their ministry. Those operating through this spirit will be focused on instilling fear and even inducing (lead, move, persuade, influence, stimulate a synthesis) fear through their blatant passive aggressive actions. This spirit only has as much power over a person if they succumb to this spirit or rise against it. Some people who operate as passive aggressive intimidators, will act as though they are exempt from any responsibility regarding their behavior. This is because they are not blatantly doing anything against the person, but subtly they are filling them with fear and persuasions that hinders forward movement in God, while abusing and bewitching you. Therefore, this spirit can be equated to mind control.

Sometimes dance leaders can operate in intimidation through dictatorship rather than a spirit of encouragement and empowerment. This is a misuse of authority, where they have absolute unrestricted control, and they are the supreme authority leaving no room for the members to have a voice, eyes (vision), and ears (hearing) in the ministry. Thus they receive minimal opportunity to grow in who they are as dance ministers. When intimidation is at work in a dance leader, it tends to be the leaders way only or no way. There is no compromise or respect for the members' giftings and callings, or perceptions. Timidity, fear, and control is used to coward the members into submission. The members tend to minister and operate from a place of dread, while feeling constantly overwhelmed and frustrated. The members will feel a need to be perfect, while living under a fear of failing, while striving to live up to the standards that are being required of them. There tends to be a lot of bickering behind the scenes as members will voice concerns among themselves and to outsiders rather than to the leader. They do this because they fear being rebuked, chastised, and not having their perceptions validated.

When a dance leader or member is challenged with a spirit of intimidation, they may be difficult to approach. The intimidator may possess strict rules and regimens about how things should go and will seek to impose those ideas on the dance team. The intimidator may be easily offended and will be good at arguing his or her point. They also may be combative and because they are good at stating their case, others will find it difficult to share an opinion or concern with them. Though this may not be their intent or heart, the person may appear prideful and abusive, because there approach tends to be harsh, strict, aggressive and abrasive. They may have bible scriptures to solidify the reasons they think or believe a certain way, yet most times, these scriptures are used out of contexts and in error to their true meaning and biblical intent. Those with issues of insecurities, shyness, etc., will be prey to such leaders and members. These members will find it difficult to stand up for themselves and will often coward under the intimidation tactics of these spirits.

Though not always the case, some people operating in the spirit of intimidation may not know it. Speaking with them privately in love about it can be key to helping them be delivered from this demonic spirit. There are also those that know it, but do not want deliverance or are not willing to be delivered. God may lead you to pray and intercede for the deliverance of a leader or member who is challenged with this demonic spirit. If you find that the spirit of intimidation is still evident within a leader and change is not their intent, it is important to explore if this is the ministry for you. God is about empowerment and liberation.   God does not require us to be cowered under anyone, as when we submit under wrong authority, they become our God or whatever they are submitted to becomes our God.

Spirits of Rebellion, Stubbornness, & Defiance Against Authority

> *1Samuel 15:23 For rebellion is as the sin of witchcraft, and stubbornness is as iniquity and idolatry. Because thou hast rejected the word of the LORD, he hath also rejected thee from being king.*

In this passage of scripture, one of the Hebrew words for *rebellion* is *"bitterness."*

Dictionary.com defines *rebellion* as:
1. open, organized, and armed resistance to one's government or ruler
2. resistance to or defiance of any authority, control, or tradition

Dictionary.com defines a *rebel* as:
1. a person who refuses allegiance to, resists, or rises in arms against the government or ruler of his or her country
2. a person who resists any authority, control, or tradition
3. rebellious, defiant

When rebellion is present, there may be a bitter root in our souls and hearts that we need to be delivered from. This bitterness sometimes stems from past experiences that we have not forgiven others for or forgiven ourselves for. When we are bitter regarding a person in authority, we will manifest that bitterness with those in leadership, even when that person has not done anything to offend us. This is because of an unhealed need to avenge ourselves of what has happened to us. But because we have a bitter root of rebellion it bewitches us into thinking our actions are okay and even justifiable. This demonic spirit gives the assumptions that we are entitled to behave rebelliously, and even makes us stubborn and idolatrous where we only think of ourselves, our feelings, needs and desires, while neglecting the good of all parties involved and/or the ministry as a whole. We become immovable, uncompromising, and self-absorbed, thus becoming an idol unto ourselves. Nothing or no one else is considered in the choices we make, as the aim is to please self and fulfill some justifiable need or desire within ourselves.

A person who is rebellious – defiant - is generally insubordinate.

Some synonym definitions from dictionary.com as it relates to being *insubordinate* are:
1. contumacious – stubbornly perverse or rebellious; willfully and obstinately disobedient
2. refractory - hard or impossible to manage, hard to fuse, resistant to ordinary methods of treatment
3. recalcitrant - noncompliant
4. rebellious, insolent; daring, resistant, challenging

People challenged by these demonic spirits will have:
- Difficulty unifying with the ministry and team members

- Resist direction and redirection
- Have challenges following or complying to the rules and regulations of the ministry
- Resist following requirements for preparing for ministry engagements
- Unifies just enough to be in the ministry but not enough to be a true team player
- Can easily fall into backsliding as they do just enough at times to comply but not enough to be truly transformed
- Will attempt to coast off his or her gifting and will get away with sins because of his or her gift, but will be a disruption and open door of bringing warfare and impurity into the ministry

Some of this will show in their movement as they will constantly get steps wrong or go the wrong way. They will have to be told constantly that they are going the wrong way or doing a move wrong. These demonic spirits tend to be lodged in the flesh and will of a person. Therefore the person may appear very stubborn, and even when they want to do right, wrong will appear at times - wrong or defiant movement will manifest.

- This person will have to be delivered and healed of past issues that caused them to give into the bitterness and unforgiveness. Many of these experiences will be related to those in authority taking advantage, neglecting, abusing, or offending them, as some injustice

has caused trauma and pain in the person's soul and heart.
- The person then will have to practice rooting rebellion out of their flesh and will. A fast may be required to subject their will under the power of their spirit.
- The person will then have to search out the reason God led them to be a part of the dance ministry and the reason God led them to submit to that dance leader. This revelation will help them be accountable to submitting to the rules and regulations of that ministry and leader. The person should also be held accountable to what God requires of them when personality traits of rebellion occur in their behavior.
- Because rebellion is rooted in the flesh and will of a person, it will take time to fully process to wholeness. The person and the leader must be willing to work together, as the process to wholeness unfolds. The person who is being delivered must be willing to accept rebuke and correction when necessary to further root this spirit out of their will and personality. Rebuke and correction should be done in love and sometimes it is best to take the person aside and speak with them versus handling the situation publicly. The goal is to bring healing and value to the person by building them up in trusting God, and trusting those he has given rule over them. Tearing down the person and embarrassing the person could further root

rebellion in them and prolong the process to wholeness.

Hebrews 13:17-18 *Obey them that have the rule over you, and submit yourselves: for they watch for your souls, as they that must give account, that they may do it with joy, and not with grief: for that is unprofitable for you. Pray for us: for we trust we have a good conscience, in all things willing to live honestly.*

Philippians 2:3 *Let nothing be done through strife or vainglory; but in lowliness of mind let each esteem other better than themselves.*

1Peter 3:8-9 *Finally, be ye all of one mind, having compassion one of another, love as brethren, be pitiful, be courteous: Not rendering evil for evil, or railing for railing: but contrariwise blessing; knowing that ye are thereunto called, that ye should inherit a blessing.*

Spirits of Murmuring and Complaining

Spirits of murmuring and complaining can oppress a minister of dance when they are angry, frustrated, agitated, tired, stressed, weary about life, about challenges concerning the ministry or regarding their kingdom walk. When spirits of murmuring and complaining set in, members can become rebellious and resistant to the rules and regulations of the ministry and the expectations and requirements that God is speaking to them personally or the ministry as a whole. They may begin complaining and murmuring about how the dance ministry is conducted, speaking against the leader, begin to find fault and voice complaints against team members, and even speaking against God and the vision of God for the ministry. Such actions can draw other team members into complaining and murmuring, while speaking against their ministry and team members.

Murmuring and complaining tends to be rooted in ill will or resentment, and the person becomes challenged by life or ministry circumstances and it causes emotional sickness, displeasure, bitterness, offense, insult, and feelings of injustice in their souls and heart. When not dealt with, this person's emotional sickness spreads and contaminate the souls and hearts of people. This spirit is contagious, and loves company, and essentially needs company and attention in order to thrive. Murmuring and complaining opens the door to sin and idolatry as people's souls and hearts begin to deny, resist, reject, or become dull to the truth, and they begin to walk in their own plans and perceptions. These plans and perceptions are often in effort to immediately satisfy the flesh and the soul and are often against the will and plans of God for their life and ministry. When this occurs, you may have members leave the ministry before their season is ended and even encouraging others to leave. They will start operating by their own rules and standards and rally people to uphold their point of view.

> ***Ephesians 4:29*** *Let no corrupt communication proceed out of your mouth, but that which is good to the use of edifying, that it may minister grace unto the hearers.*

<u>Corrupt</u> in the Greek is *sapros* and means:
1. rotten, i.e. worthless (literally or morally): — bad, corrupt
2. putrefied corrupted by one and no longer fit for use
3. worn out, of poor quality, unfit for use

Philippians 2:4 *Do all things without grumbling and faultfinding and complaining [against God] and questioning and doubting [among yourselves], That you may show yourselves to be blameless and guileless, innocent and uncontaminated, children of God without blemish (faultless, unrebukable) in the midst of a crooked and wicked generation [spiritually perverted and perverse], among whom you are seen as bright lights (stars or beacons shining out clearly) in the [dark] world.*

Spirits of Competition & Comparison

The spirit of competition can operate consciously or unconsciously within a person or a dance ministry. This spirit can also be very overt or subtle, depending on who it is manifesting through. It can operate through the most prideful person or the most shy, insecure person.

The spirit of competition will have a person competing with the leader or with team members. This demonic spirit will have a person competing in their mind as they are plagued with thoughts of needing to be seen, perfect, or better than everyone else. This person may strive to change moves that have been set or that are needed for the ministry piece. Their reason will be more in effort to outdo others than truly having revelation that benefits the dance piece.

The spirit of competition manifested among the disciples. In **Matthew 18:1-6, Luke 9:46-48, and Luke 22:24-27**, we find the disciples asking Jesus who is the greatest in the kingdom of heaven. Jesus pulled a child close to him and expressed that unless we come unto him as children, we will not inherit the kingdom of heaven no matter how great we are. Jesus went on to express that if we offend or cause one another to sin or stumble in our conduct or thought we will be judged harshly. He then stated that the humble is the greatest among us all.

Jesus encourages us to be cautious with entertaining such thoughts and actions. Whether intentional or unintentional, conscious or unconscious, when the spirit of competition is at work, it breeds sin and stumbling in the conduct and thoughts of others. The spirit of competition draws others into competing, comparing, challenging, becoming jealous and envious, while causing discord and strife on to another. Even those who may not be participating are now having thoughts of whether they are adequate and living up to par. It is important for leaders to be discerning of when this spirit is surfacing and it is important for dance members to cast down thoughts of competition, and deal with underlying issues of inadequacies and insecurity that cause these spirits to have an open door in their lives.

All movement flows through our gifts and callings, therefore, we may minister the same movement, but it manifests according to who we are in God. It is important for each dance member to know their gifts and callings and how they impact the dance ministry and impact each particular dance engagement. This will also aide in dismantling competition and comparison spirits as you are focused on God's purpose for you and glorifying God rather than fulfilling your own insecurities, while glorifying self.

> *Galatians 5:23-26 The Amplified Bible*
> *Gentleness (meekness, humility), self-control (self-restraint, continence). Against such things there is no law [that can bring a charge]. And those who belong to Christ Jesus (the Messiah) have crucified*

> the flesh (the godless human nature) with its passions and appetites and desires. If we live by the [Holy] Spirit, let us also walk by the Spirit. [If by the Holy Spirit we have our life in God, let us go forward walking in line, our conduct controlled by the Spirit.] Let us not become vainglorious and self-conceited, competitive and challenging and provoking and irritating to one another, envying and being jealous of one another.

If you are a dance minister who has received technical training from the world, you have competed in dance competitions, battles, have participated in dance auditions and etc., it is important that you cleanse from these experiences, because they produce a spirit of competition and comparison. This section is not to speak negatively toward technical dancing, and technical dance training schools and centers, as it is a great asset. This section is to bring enlightenment on how to adequately cleanse oneself from the negative influence that dancing in the world, and in competitive dance arenas. The atmosphere of worldly dance, competitive dance, and dance auditions is one of competition, comparison, perfection, and measuring yourself against others to be better than them in order to win an award, gain acceptance into a college, or arts program, and gain the accolades and praises of a teacher. Although you may not have been one to manifest this spirit, when you were dancing in these settings your dancing was soaked and cultivated in these spirits, and so it needs to be cleansed out such that there is no manifestation of this in your ministry.

Past teachers who taught you technical or competitive dance may have critiqued you while comparing you to others, pressured you to be like others, worked you to perfection, which then birthed a spirit of competition and comparison in you. If you were one who participated in dance auditions, the audition process also engrained these spirits into you, because auditioning is rooted in comparing everyone for the purposes of choosing who is the best. There are instances where they place dancers head to head with one another, and even write down what they believe is good and bad about your dancing. Such critiques can be very hurtful. It is very important to cleanse these things out of your dance, out of your identity, and self-image, as they can have a major influence on healthy self-confidence, self-esteem, and acceptance.

Often in technical dance and dancing for the world, body types are harshly critiqued. The dancer is expected to maintain a certain physique and weight. Flexibility is measured, and if the dancer does not have a certain level of flexibility, they are looked down upon. The dancer is told that they will not go as far and be as successful as those who are flexible. Moreover, a dancer's feet are critiqued, and if you do not have a certain type of arch in your foot, they also will tell you that your dancing capabilities and success will be limited. These things may have caused you to strive to be someone else, take pieces of someone else, work to perfection, cause you to have a distorted body image, or cause you to feel bad about yourself. It steals your originality and identity, your desire to dance, thus potentially thwarting the call of dance on your life. These experiences need to be gutted and cleansed out of your soul and dance calling so that you can operate in the purity of your calling. Please understand that your uniqueness and individuality matters. We were not built the same. We all have different callings, mantles, and purposes to fulfill, and our design is all a part of that. We cannot carry the mindsets of the world's dance culture into ministry because the things of the world have no value in the kingdom. The world is set up on the concepts of who is better, getting ahead, and being dogmatic. Therefore, competition and comparison is a part of the nature of the world, and those spirits strengthen you to be successful in society. But they are unnecessary in the kingdom because we are already successful. God has made us great, we all are important, valuable, and the best that God has created us to be to fulfill His purpose and plan for our lives.

Mocking Spirits

> ***Proverbs 3:34*** *Surely he scorneth (mocks) the scorners (mockers): but he giveth grace unto the lowly.*

<u>*Scorneth* and *Scorners* in this scripture is the Hebrew word *lus* and means:</u>
1. properly, to make mouths at, i.e. to scoff
2. hence (from the effort to pronounce a foreign language) to interpret, or (generally) intercede

3. ambassador, have in derision, interpreter, make a mock, mocker, scorn(-er, -ful), teacher
4. to be inflated, act as a scorner, show oneself as a mocker

Essentially when you are mocking others, you are servicing as an intercessor, ambassador, teacher that is thus training others how to disrespect someone or something. It is okay to laugh and have fun in our interactions and practices. It is however, important to be careful in not making comments that belittle, ridicule, abuse, and devalue your team members. It is especially important to not become so familiar where you just make blatant hurtful comments that may or may not be funny, yet lack regard for how the person is perceiving them or taking offense to them.

We must be honest in recognizing that some jokes are really disguised abuse or are our heart issues manifesting the truth of what we feel, think or believe. Mocking Spirits are a quick hang out in the atmosphere and culture of dance ministries or relationship interactions so they can take advantage of opportunities of familiarity and lack of regard. They tend to strike when it is least expected, while using mimicking, quick whit, judgmental comments, harsh or blatant jokes to cause offense, strife and division.

The mocking spirit actually births division as one of the definitions of mock is too attack. When someone is under attack it is them against whatever is attacking. They are not on the same side. As dance ministers and team members, we are on the same team. We are one body with different members. We are an army. When operating in the mocking spirit, we are attacking one another and opening the door for a spirit of division to infiltrate. We are also hiding behind jokes and laughs that are throwing darts at another person. It is like the hidden way of saying what you truly want to say about your issues and challenges with a person, rather than dealing with those challenges and issues in a healthy manner. By handling things in a healthy manner, mature conversation and resolution can take place, and true change can occur, instead of getting secret satisfaction through mocking and ridiculing a person, while drawing others into doing it as well.

One of the synonyms of scorn is contempt. When you are treating someone with contempt you are being mean, vial (repulsive, disgusting, filthy, foul), and worthless. It is an act of showing disrespect, and dishonor. We may not think of this or be mindful of this when we are having fun, joking, and playing games, but we are actually disrespecting, dishonoring, taunting, treating someone as if they are worthless, and putting them down. This is unacceptable as we should be esteeming one another higher than we esteem ourselves.

Another word for mock is mimic. When we are mimicking others we are copying and imitating another person's actions, the things that they say, how they behave and etc. and essentially we are making fun of and ridiculing who a person is. We are also making fun of their personality, their attributes, and how they may express themselves and interact. This can cause much harm to a person, by making them feel rejected, isolated, bullied, inferior, and inadequate. They may begin to self-reject and self-isolate to avoid the ridicule. They may become offended, withdrawn, and wounded. They may feel abused amongst those who should be loving them, encouraging, edifying, comforting, and building them up rather than tearing them down. We cannot give the enemy any room to infiltrate by allowing the mocking spirit to hide behind jokes, fun and games, and laughs that really abuse, harm, and wound others.

We must be sensitive to the Holy Spirit so he can bring correction when we have crossed a line with people or just in general. Be humble enough to repent quickly when there is an unction in your spirit that something you said or did may have offended, been misinterpreted or could have become an open door to strife or division. When you feel convicted, even if that person or team does not hold you accountable, hold yourself accountable, by repenting to the person and even the team if necessary.

Leaders must also hold themselves and team members to this standard as when mocking spirits invade the ministry, it breaches safety and trust. Members then start to feel unsafe and as if they cannot trust the members and the ministry with their insecurities, weaknesses, fears, shortcomings. The ministry should be a safe place to grow, but the operating of this spirit makes it battling ground rather than safe ground, and as people step onto the ground to come forth in who they are, learn, and grow, they are getting shot down, and killed in a place where they should be coming alive and awakening; where they should feel safe to not have to guard themselves and be free to be who they are as they learn and grow more in God and who God is in them. This spirit actually sabotages a person's growth because it makes them feel uncomfortable to be themselves and to take strides out of fear of being mocked and ridiculed, so instead they stop stretching out to learn and grow because they are guarding and shielding themselves from this spirit. It also sabotages relationships in this same manner because the person becomes guarded and no longer comfortable to just be themselves, and they become abused and wounded in the relationship and eventually the relationship perishes and we see people disconnecting from the ministry that should have been helping them to grow and connect to God. I also believe that this spirit causes church hurt, and it sends people away from the church and away from God when truly this spirit and these actions are not a representation or true depiction of the church and who God is.

We must make sure that our ministries are cultivated with the nature and character of who God is and a spirit of love, honor and respect where people feel they can be empowered and grow. Therefore, address mocking spirits quickly by repenting and forgiving one another. The more you practice this, the more it will become a part of your ministry culture. God will also honor the humility of team members and the ministry, and there will be an increase of power and anointing that will flow through the deep unity that radiates within the team.

> ***Matthew 18:15*** *Moreover if thy brother shall trespass against thee, go and tell him his fault between thee and him alone: if he shall hear thee, thou hast gained thy brother.*
>
> ***Luke 17:3*** *Take heed to yourselves: If thy brother trespass against thee, rebuke him; and if he repent, forgive him.*
>
> ***1Peter 3:8-9 The Amplified Bible*** *Finally, all [of you] should be of one and the same mind (united in spirit), sympathizing [with one another], loving [each other] as brethren [of one household], compassionate and courteous (tenderhearted and humble). Never return evil for evil or insult for insult (scolding, tongue-lashing, berating), but on the contrary blessing [praying for their welfare, happiness, and protection, and truly pitying and loving them]. For know that to this you have been called, that you may yourselves inherit a blessing [from God – that you may obtain a blessing as heirs, bringing welfare and happiness and protection].*

Spirit of Pride

The dancer who operates in pride may want to lead all the time or be in the front. They may overly volunteer for leads and dance pieces and speak against others who are striving to grow and come forth in their dance ministry. This dancer will seek out accolades and praise then will make comments to further promote personal praise. They tend to be glory stealers and self- idolaters as they will be focused on what they did within a ministry piece or engagement, versus how God was glorified through the entire team. Many with the spirit of pride will also embellish stories, lie, and even lie on God to make themselves or an experience be greater or more awe striking than it really is.

> ***Proverbs 16:5*** *Every one [that is] proud in heart [is] an abomination to the LORD: [though] hand [join] in hand, he shall not be unpunished.*
>
> ***James 4:6*** *But he giveth more grace. Wherefore he saith, God resisteth the proud, but giveth grace unto the humble.*
>
> ***Isaiah 42:8*** *I am the Lord: that is my name: and my glory will I not give to another, neither my praise to graven images.*

Many prideful people are insecure. Pride is a mask to hide secret feelings and thoughts of inadequacy, low self-esteem, and self-worth. The prideful person tend to be overbearing and self-absorbed in his or her strengths and successes in effort to prevent these identity issues from being exposed.

> ***1Corinthians 4:18-20*** *Now some are puffed up, as though I would not come to you. But I will come to you shortly, if the Lord will, and will know, not the speech of them which are puffed up, but the power.*

> *For the kingdom of God is not in word, but in power.*

If not dealt with, pride can cause a destruction and even a falling away where restoration is not possible.

> **Proverbs 16:18** *Pride [goeth] before destruction, and an haughty spirit before a fall.*
>
> **Proverbs 29:23** *A man's pride shall bring him low: but honour shall uphold the humble in spirit.*

God requires humility. In order for a dancer to truly embody the presence of God where lives are transformed through their ministry, he or she must be gracious, meek, and humble. Because dancing is a spotlight ministry where we are before the people, we must constantly check ourselves for the spirit of pride. It is very easy to yield to spirits of pride and not even know it. Especially when ministry engagements increase, notoriety increases, and people are approaching you after ministry and bestowing blessings and accolades upon you. We must be careful in recognizing that we are not performers or entertainers. We are ministers of God. Therefore, it is important to be cautious and repent for any subtle pride or lack of humility. Even be willing to have others speak truth to you regarding this area and pursue counsel of those who can examine you with a spiritual perception and aide you in humbling yourself under God when necessary.

As a ministry regularly renounce the spirit of pride when you all are praying as a team. Commit to not giving it any room in your life and ministry. The more the ministry is submitted and humble before God, the greater praise, worship, and movement can exude with power from your ministry.

> *1Peter 5:6 The Amplified Bible Therefore humble yourselves [demote, lower yourselves in your own estimation] under the mighty hand of God, that in due time He may exalt you.*

Spirit of Betrayal

Sometimes there will be a person in the ministry that may be planted by the enemy to betray the leader or the ministry team. Spirits of betrayal are not uncommon and should not shock us, for **Matthew 24:10** says, *And then shall many be offended, and shall betray one another, and shall hate one another.* If you are successful then you will experience betrayal at different levels of your ministry. There is really no way to avoid spirits of betrayal. We can try to prepare for them but doing so causes us to be guarded in our interactions, and accusatory towards those who mean well towards us. We are not able to relax in our interactions because we fear being hurt, berated, and assaulted by the very ones we are to love and esteem. We should be conscious that betrayal may occur through the most unlikely of persons. And though you can never prepare for betrayal, here are some keys that can be utilized when exploring the spirit of betrayal. I would also encourage you to study the story of Judas and Jesus (*Luke 22*) for further assistance in identifying and dealing with spirits of betrayal.

- The betrayer is often self-serving and seeking to prosper in finances or position. The challenge is the betrayer is willing to sell you out to get his or her needs or desires met.
- Whether conscious or unconscious, the betrayer wants to be you and will seek to replace you. I say unconscious because some insecure or inadequate people tend to be subject to the spirit of betrayal and not even realize it until they have betrayed you. Their desire to replace you will be by way of selling you out or eliminating you in some way where they can defile or diminish your reputation and take your place.
- The betrayer is usually operating in carefully crafted words where they appear as if they are for you and are invested in what God is doing in your life and in the ministry. Or maybe they are but their insecurities cause them to be an open door to steal your heart then stab you in it.
- The betrayer operates in a projected loyalty or even in a pure loyalty. They can walk with you and the ministry for seasons and even be your personal confidant. They may give you beneficial wise counsel, flatter you with kind and encouraging words, and even prophecy into your life. It will appear or be as if they are very supporting and that they see what God desires to do in your life and in the ministry.
- The challenge with this is during the times where you or the ministry are in a vulnerable

state or a season of transitioning or elevation, you do not realize that the betrayer is not for you.
- Something may shift in them or nothing shifts, but the truth of who they are will begin to reveal itself. One major key is the relationship with you and/or the ministry shifts, which is where the betrayal begins.
- Again please know that you cannot escape betrayal so even as it is unfolding, it must continue in order for the fullness of your transition and/or the ministry's transition to take place. All of the actions of the betrayer are calculated and covered by false loyalty, and often go unnoticed until the moment of the blatant act of betrayal. Therefore it is no way to stop the betrayal because it has intertwined itself with the process of the transition. This is the reason I contend that some experiences people call betrayal are not betrayal. When betrayal really occurs, the consequences cannot be changed. Betrayal unleashes a series of events that cannot be stopped, and that goes for all parties involved.
- The betrayer may not even realize their actions until they see the consequences, and even then the betrayer may not care or take responsibility for how their actions impact you and the ministry.

The main challenge with dealing with those who operate in a spirit of betrayal is that it causes a breach in covenant. There can be reconciliation where forgiveness and healing of hurts occur, however, the covenant cannot be restored to its original state. The issue of trust will always be a factor, therefore, a new covenant has to be made to bring security to the betrayal never occurring again. And even then it takes an abundance of work on both parties to restore the relationship. Sometimes, there is one person that is not willing to do what it takes to build a new covenant so even if these relationships are reconciled, the relationships are never restored. There also has to be the realization in that the person or ministry being betrayed enters a new place, so in order for the betrayer to unify with that person or ministry again, it has to be on the new level, as that person or ministry is not who they were and where they used to be once the betrayal unfolds and the transition is complete.

Regardless to whether you know who is going to betray you like Jesus did, or you are caught off guard, I liken the pain of betrayal to someone who was a friend or loyal foe, coming up and stabbing you in the heart. You now feel tricked, led astray, confused, and exposed to everyone. You do not know who to trust and so all kinds of thoughts and feelings flood your heart and soul as shock and trauma overtakes you. It is important however, not to get caught up in vindicating or defending yourself and or the ministry, while being so focused on the experience of betrayal that you and/or the ministry do not continue forward in transitioning to where God is taking you. Even in the midst of the pain, it is essential to press onward as God unveils victory on your behalf.

Romans 12:19 *Dearly beloved, avenge not yourselves, but rather give place unto wrath: for it is written, Vengeance is mine; I will repay, saith the Lord.*

<u>Overcoming Betrayal</u>
- Spend time acknowledging and releasing all anger, rage, pain, hurt, shock and awe, slander, trickery, dishonor, false loyalty, manipulation, lies, deceitful control, need to vindicate and defend self, offense to God and cleanse these attributes out of your heart and soul by applying the blood of Jesus.
- Forgive the betrayer and all parties involved; release the situation itself to God.
- Cast out the spirit of betrayal, murder, shock and awe, trauma, pain, mistrust, confusion, untruths that is lodged in your soul and heart.
- Cast out all demonic spirits of division and disunion operating between you and other people or you and the ministry. These spirits tend to be lodged in the spirit realm and intertwined in the atmosphere of those parties involved, and where the betrayal occurred.
- Break the power of bewitchment and memory recall, and cleanse out the power of triggers that cause you to relive the situation over and over in your mind.
- Cleanse out all daggers and stabbing sensations and impressions.
- Ask God to heal your heart and soul such that the feelings of vulnerability and exposure are fused.

- Fill your soul and heart with God's love, acceptance, truth, and confidence.
- Spend time decreeing out who God says you are and the truth of who he says you are, and who and what he has called you to be.

You may have to complete these prayer steps multiple times to really heal your heart and soul of the effects of betrayal.

Spirits of Performance and Entertainment

As dance ministers and dance ministries, we must know that we are not performers and entertainers. We must not allow others to make us performers and entertainers by using us to fill in programs, be on display at their events, patty cake us as if we are some secular entertainer with no godly power. It is important to know that we embody the word, presence, and will of God. We come to release, reveal, and establish the kingdom of God in people, places, and ministries. We must seek God for His purpose for a ministry engagement and only attend at his leading. We must be sound in his biblical word and truth, and cultivated in a relationship with him so that our movements set us apart from performers and entertainers. We must know our giftings and callings and live and minister through that anointing so that people will not box us in as dance performers and entertainers. We must regularly fast, pray, train, exercise, eat healthy, and submit our bodies to him as living sacrifices such that we yield no offense to our gifting and calling of dance and to God. And so that our disciplines separate us from the world's ways and standards regarding dance.

Romans 12:1-2 *The Amplified Bible I APPEAL to you therefore, brethren, and beg of you in view of [all] the mercies of God, to make a decisive dedication of your bodies [presenting all your members and faculties] as a living sacrifice, holy (devoted, consecrated) and well pleasing to God, which is your reasonable (rational, intelligent) service and spiritual worship. Do not be conformed to this world (this age), [fashioned after and adapted to its external, superficial customs], but be transformed (changed) by the [entire] renewal of your mind [by its new ideals and its new attitude], so that you may prove [for yourselves] what is the good and acceptable and perfect will of God, even the thing which is good and acceptable and perfect [in His sight for you].*

It is so important to note that our bodies are not our own and that sanctification is our greatest weapon against being set apart from the world and the spirits of performance and entertainment.

> **1Corinthians 6:18-20** *Flee fornication. Every sin that a man doeth is without the body; but he that committeth fornication sinneth against his own body. What? know ye not that your body is the temple of the Holy Ghost which is in you, which ye have of God, and ye are not your own? For ye are bought with a price: therefore glorify God in your body, and in your spirit, which are God's.*

<u>Fornication</u> in this scripture is the Greek word *porneuō* and means:

1. to act the harlot, i.e. (literally) indulge unlawful lust (of either sex), or (figuratively) practice idolatry, commit fornication
2. to prostitute one's body to the lust of another
3. to give one's self to unlawful sexual intercourse
4. to be given to idolatry, to worship idols
5. to permit one's self to be drawn away by another into idolatry

We see from the definition that fornication does not just include sexual sin. When we prostitute our bodies - our gift and calling of dance - for the lust of others who want to make money, fame, acquire notoriety or gain success off us, we are fornicating against God. When we give into entertainment and performance spirits whether in the church or in the world, we are being drawn away by another into idolatry and we are worshipping idols.

As those who have the true vision of what dance ministry really is, we have to teach this to others, and bring them into the revelation that we have. Dance has been used and displayed continuously as a source of performance and entertainment in and outside of the church, so the people who we are ministering to may already have preconceived notion concerning our ministry. We have to be ready and open to teach people the truth concerning dance ministry and our assignment at hand.

Many times we may minister in places that believe dance is a source of entertainment and performance. They may sit down on the ministry and not be very enthusiastic about it because we are not entertaining them. During these engagements, it is very easy to become challenged, discouraged, frustrated, or angry with the people, because we want them to receive and be engaged. Yet it is important that we cleanse from these emotions, and be willing to teach the people, and be firm and focused in knowing that we are not responsible for entertaining and making them happy. They are responsible for receiving what God is speaking through our ministry for themselves. They should have a focus to connect with God and what he is doing as we minister. They need to know that dance ministry brings transformation, healing, deliverance, and releases a word from the Lord into their lives, it is not to appease them. At one point we too had to gain revelation on the truth of dance ministry, and so we too have to be okay with the process that others have to go through to come into the fullness of the revelation of what dance ministry truly is.

 Others can expect entertainment and performance from us, but we also can set ourselves in this position, where we minister looking to receive the praise and accolades of people. It is a blessing to receive words of encouragement and affirmation from those we minister to, but that should not be our focus as we minister. We are not dancing to please and gain a positive response from people like performers do. Our focus should be on the word that God gave us to minister, while trusting him to honor and bless us for the work that we do for him. We need to be rooted in knowing that we are God's vessels, who release, establish, plant, and impart his word into people, atmospheres, regions, and territories. Our ministry is not about charming, indulging, or pleasing others. SHIFT!

Spirit of Offense
This spirit can work amongst a team through members taking offense to correction, constructive criticisms, pure jokes (not meant for harm), conversations, and etc., when their intention was not to be offensive but to have healthy communication and interaction with the person. This spirit can operate between leader and member, and member and member. It is difficult to communicate with a person operating in this spirit, because you never know what will trigger offense. This person typically becomes offended without warning. The leader will try to give this person correction, and constructive criticism, but the person will immediately feel as though they are being wronged, attacked, and that an injustice is being done to them. Also if the team is sharing laughs, jokes, and conversations that include the person, and they perceive that these things are geared to harm them, they will become offended and feel like the team is ganging up on them, and bullying them. This causes division within the team, because the offended person always feels as though it is the leader and the team members against them. Yet the team accepts them and wants to embrace them, but the walls created by offense keep them at a distance.

The leader and members interacting with this person will feel as though they are being accused, as they are generally made out to be the suspect, while the person manifesting the spirit is always the victim. But truly in this instance the offended person has become the offender. The leaders and members may shut down and not want to interact and have relationship with this person, or they may continuously go on an unnecessary search within themselves trying to figure out what they are doing wrong, when really it is not their issue. It is the person's issue or rather, the spirit of offense at work.

There are instances where a person manifesting this spirit will not know they are offended. They will contend they are being wronged and attacked. But often they are reliving or filtering through past hurtful experiences as they are interacting with others. They truly are being offended and hurt all over again by the past that they have not let go of and are still bound in. They are not being offended by the team, and the team should not take responsibility for their past experiences. Be sensitive to discerning this spirit because it will drain you, have you confused, wondering what is wrong, and searching yourself unnecessarily. When yielding to this pattern of behavior, you will become just as bound as the person with the offensive spirit.

This spirit operates through:
- Miscommunication & misperception - where the person continually misunderstands what is being said and communicated with them.
- Unhealed issues of the past where they have been abused, ridiculed, bullied and truly

offended, but they are harboring this offense and reflecting it upon you when you say something that reminds them and takes them back to this offense.
- Triggers - words and actions that remind them of things that happened in the past that take them back to reliving the past offenses.
- Insecurities, inadequacies, and low self-esteem that has come in through past offenses, experiences, abuse
- Victim spirit

Teaching and demonstrating how to express ones' feelings, concerns and how to resolve conflict is key to bringing healing to someone with the spirit of offense. They may be surprised at what is being discussed because of their justifications, but speak truth to them in love, because they need to be free. This will also provide an avenue for them and the entire team to engage in healthy communication and conflict resolution skills.

This person also needs to go through a deliverance process, where they are cleansed from all past offense, bitterness, unforgiveness, anger, abuse, ridicule, bullying, and triggers that cause them to revisit the past. In addition, the person may need deliverance from unhealthy perception, poor or confused hearing, and judging situations through a negative well. This will be a process, as this spirit can be deeply rooted and enmeshed in a person's personality, character, and behaviors. They will need much love, patience, and encouragement while they process through to wholeness. They will also need someone to help them walk this out. Having a mentor or counselor will aid in the deliverance, because this will break the mindset it is them against everyone else. They will see that they have people that are with them, they will not feel alone, and the walls of offense can begin to be broken down.

> **Proverbs 18:19** *A brother offended is harder to be won than a strong city: and their contentions are like the bars of a castle.*
>
> **Leviticus 19:18** *Thou shalt not avenge, nor bear any grudge against the children of thy people, but thou shalt love thy neighbour as thyself:I am the Lord.*
>
> **1 Thessalonians 5:11-13 New Living Translation** *Wherefore comfort yourselves together, and edify one another, even as also ye do. And we beseech you, brethren, to know them which labour among you, and are over you in the Lord, and admonish you; And to esteem them very highly in love for their work's sake. And be at peace among yourselves.*
>
> **1 Thessalonians 5:15 New Living Translation** *See that none render evil for evil unto any man; but ever follow that which is good, both among yourselves, and to all men.*

Spirit of Defense
Defense in Dictionary.com means:
1. resistance against attack; protection
2. something that defends as a fortification, physical or mental quality, or medication
3. the defending of a cause or the like by speech, argument, etc.
4. the denial or pleading of the defendant

This spirit operates through self-protection. If a person is manifesting this spirit they will feel as though what is being spoken has the potential to cause them harm, so they will immediately become defensive in order to protect and shield themselves. This spirit can manifest when the leader is giving correction, instruction, and constructive criticism. But it will also manifests in general conversation, and when the leader and team members are interacting and communicating with this person. This spirit operates frequently through fear, insecurity, and pride. But it is all in means to self-protect.

Different ways the spirit of defense manifests:
- Fear - as they fear being hurt. They protect themselves because things remind them of past hurts that they have received through harsh, hurtful experiences with past leaders, their peers, or those who have had some type of authority over their lives.
- Insecurity - due to them not being secure in who they are, they will become defensive in times where they feel like they have to assert

and prove to you, the team members, and even themselves who they are.
- Pride & haughtiness- as they will be in denial if they do not agree with whatever you are sharing with them. They will feel as though they are always doing everything correctly and that they don't need any correction. This will make it difficult for the leader to interact and communicate with this person because they will become defensive when the leader gives them correction and instruction on how to improve and better themselves. And if the team is trying to help them during practice, they will also respond to them in this same manner. The team will find it hard to unify and work as a team with this person, because they can become defensive no matter what is said.

A person dealing with this spirit will have a hard time receiving from people, therefore, pride, insecurity, and/or fear will need to be cleansed. Due to a lack of reception, this person has difficulty growing personally in their gifting, and this also challenges their growth with the team. The person may not recognize that they operate in this spirit. This spirit can be embedded in a person's personality, behaviors, and identity. They need to submit to mentoring and the process of deliverance and healing. They require truth throughout the process to keep them accountable and honest. They need to be cleansed from fear and the past where they were abused, criticized harshly, and mistreated by leaders, parents, peers, or any authority figure where they felt defenseless. All word curses and pacts they made in saying that they would never be defenseless again, and that they would protect and defend themselves need to be broken. All revenge seeking, and wanting to avenge themselves from their hurtful experiences, harboring the past through unforgiveness and bitterness needs to be cleansed. They need to be cleansed from any insecurity, and healed to a place of wholeness within themselves where they understand that who they are will speak for itself, and who they are is great in the Lord. They need to be cleansed from strongholds that cause wrong thinking and feelings that the corrections and help of others diminishes who they are, because it actually enhances it. Moreover, they need to completely relinquish all rights to protect and shield themselves, and receive healing in trusting, and relying on God as their protector and shield.

> ***Psalms 5:11-12*** *But let all those that put their trust in thee rejoice: let them ever shout for joy, because thou defendest them: let them also that love thy name be joyful in thee. For thou, Lord, wilt bless the righteous; with favour wilt thou compass him as with a shield.*
>
> ***Psalms 36:7*** *How excellent is thy lovingkindness, O God!*
> *therefore the children of men put their trust under the shadow of thy wings.*
>
> ***2Samuel 22:2-3*** *And he said, The Lord is my rock, and my fortress, and my deliverer; The God of my*

> rock; in him will I trust: he is my shield, and the horn of my salvation, my high tower, and my refuge, my saviour; thou savest me from violence.

Spirit of Perfection

A person operating in this spirit will be very hard on themselves because they will always be striving to reach an unrealistic standard and level of perfection. In God we operate in his spirit of excellence where he is perfecting us; but through a spirit of perfection, we strive through our own strength, and through our own standards to perfect ourselves. We cannot be perfect within ourselves, because it is God who perfects us.

A person manifesting this spirit will become easily frustrated, sensitive, and hard on themselves if they cannot get things right the first time, and if you correct and give them instructions. If they cannot get the movements right immediately, this is viewed as imperfection. If you give them correction they hear this as you telling them that they are not perfect. They will feel as though they have failed and are displeasing you, when truly their need for unrealistic perfection has caused them to forget the reality that a learning process is natural.

The leader and team members may be hesitant to talk to this person, and very cautious as they try to find the best way to speak to them such that they can receive in a healthy manner. The leader and team members will not want them to be so hard on themselves, and will not want them to feel bad. This will become a burden to the leader and team members because it is an extra task in having to take the time to figure out how to talk to this person where they can receive, yet not succumbing to the spirit of perfection that they operate in. It will also become a burden to the person manifesting the spirit because they will be operating out of their own strength, and always striving and working extremely hard to reach their unrealistic standard of perfection. It will become extremely tiresome, weighty, unnecessary pressure on them, and it can cause anxiety. However, you do want and need to speak truth to them so that they recognize that they are operating in their strength and not God's ability to perfect that which concerns them.

The spirit of perfection is a threefold cord that consists of perfection, shame, and guilt. When the person sees the imperfection or it is revealed to them by another person, they become ashamed about it, and then begin to feel guilty about not being able to be perfect. And then in a means to do away with the shame and guilt of not being perfect, the person will then focus on striving to perfect themselves, so that they no longer feel ashamed and guilty. Where there is a spirit of perfection there is always shame and guilt making the person feel bad, discouraged, and low about themselves. Shame and guilt also reinforces the person to cycle in perfecting themselves. It causes the person to go around and around in a circle striving for perfection. As soon as they see the imperfection, they want to fix it. They will never be perfect which is the reason they need

God. If we were perfect, there would be no point in having relationship with God.

Communication, love, and a processing of deliverance and healing is needed to root out the spirit of perfection. The person needs to be cleansed of false realities and standards of perfection and the words of others that embedded this spirit where they felt as though they had to be perfect because others expected them to be. They need to be cleansed of fearing failure, being displeasing, and from feeling ashamed and guilty about not being able to perfect themselves. The threefold cord of perfection, shame, and guilt needs to be broken. And they need to receive the truth that they cannot be perfect within themselves, but only God can be their perfecter.

> ***Psalms 18:30-35*** *As for God, his way is perfect: the word of the Lord is tried: he is a buckler to all those that trust in him. For who is God save the Lord? or who is a rock save our God? It is God that girdeth me with strength, and maketh my way perfect. He maketh my feet like hinds 'feet, and setteth me upon my high places. He teacheth my hands to war, so that a bow of steel is broken by mine arms. Thou hast also given me the shield of thy salvation: and thy right hand hath holden me up, and thy gentleness hath made me great.*
>
> ***Psalms 138:8*** *The Lord will perfect that which concerneth me: thy mercy, O Lord, endureth for ever: forsake not the works of thine own hands.*

Hebrews 13:20-21 *Now the God of peace, that brought again from the dead our Lord Jesus, that great shepherd of the sheep, through the blood of the everlasting covenant, Make you perfect in every good work to do his will, working in you that which is wellpleasing in his sight, through Jesus Christ; to whom be glory for ever and ever. Amen.*

SPIRITS THAT ATTACK DANCE MANTLES & CALLINGS

JEALOUSY SPIRITS OPERATING IN DANCERS & DANCE MINISTRY

Even though David did nothing to promote himself, in *1Samuel 18:7*, we find a group of women singing of how David killed tens of thousands while Saul killed thousands.

> And the women sang to one another as they played, and said, Saul has slain his thousands, and David his ten thousands.

This song caused a spirit of jealousy and division to operate between David and his leader Saul. These spirits were allowed to enter because Saul battled with personal insecurity and inadequacy. This caused Saul to be immature in being able to handle David's anointing and success, so rather than empower him, he sought to kill the destiny and gifting that was upon David's life.

We see this a lot in ministry in general, but especially in dance ministry. Dancers may have a different dance anointing or style than their leader or other team members. Onlookers will acknowledge this, and some insecure leaders will become jealous and attack the dance minister for things others are speaking or acknowledging about the dance minister. This will first cause division within the leader and/or team members, and that person. Then an attack of assassination will begin to occur against that dance minister as they are now ostracized and at war against the very ones that should be empowering, blessing, and cultivating the anointing upon their lives. Their own leader and sometimes team members become their enemy and they find themselves having to leave to protect themselves from being taken out by their own camp. I cannot begin to explain how much hurt this has brought many people in the body of Christ. This behavior has caused people to backslide, and even has caused some to enter the secular world, while using their talents for the devil rather than God.

SPIRIT OF THE COPYCAT AS IT RELATES TO DANCE GARMENTS

When David was preparing to fight Goliath, King Saul attempts to dress David in his armor.

> ***1Samuel 17:38-40*** *And Saul armed David with his armour, and he put an helmet of brass upon his head; also he armed him with a coat of mail. And David girded his sword upon his armour, and he assayed to go; for he had not proved it. And David said unto Saul, I cannot go with these; for I have not proved them. And David put them off him. And he took his staff in his hand, and chose him five smooth stones out of the brook, and put them in a shepherd's bag which he had, even in a scrip; and his sling was in his hand: and he drew near to the Philistine.*

Armor in this passage of scripture means *"garment, judgment, raiment, clothes, or stature."* David refused to wear Saul's armor because he had not prove it. This meant that he had not tested the armor. This was interesting because David had been anointed king in *1Samuel 16:11-13*, and had a chance to wear the king's garments in war, but he recognized that he was not ready for the mantle and armor of a king, and had not achieved such qualification and prestige.

In the secular world, there are clothing styles and apparels that one person may be able to wear, yet it may not look as well on another person. The clothes we choose may also have to do with our age, financial status, culture, region, nation, the trends, creativity and taste. However, to God, clothing encompasses more than these attributes. Clothing represents our armor in the spirit and as we consider the definition of *armor*, they also are given to us based on judgment, our ability to judge, our stature, and authority in the spirit realm.

Often times, as dance ministers we will wear, borrow, or mimic the garments of other ministers. This results in looking like copycats of other dance ministers, rather than originals of ourselves and our own unique gifting and calling. We wear a beautiful garment that does not fit our body type, the dance mantle on our lives, the authority we have in the spirit, or is not conducive to the ministry piece we are ministering. We look beautiful but the fit of armor is not appropriate because we do not know what our spiritual armor looks like, and have not sought God for revelation of the mantle and armor that is on our lives; or we have on someone else's armor and armor style.

Dictionary.com defines *stature* as, *"degree of development attained, level of achievement."* If David would have worn Saul's armor, he would have come under the level of achievement and development of Saul, and what had been obtained through Saul's armor, rather than his own development and achievements. David's developments and achievements were destined and designed to exceed that of Saul's stature and authority. Therefore, if he had worn his armor, David would have come under a limited capacity and ability. Whose authority and stature have you subjected yourself to by wearing their garments and garment styles, rather than seeking God for your own garments?????

In **1Samuel 17:2-10**, we find the army of Saul afraid to come out and face Goliath.

> *And Saul and the men of Israel were gathered together, and pitched by the valley of Elah, and set the battle in array against the Philistines. And the Philistines stood on a mountain on the one side, and Israel stood on a mountain on the other side: and there was a valley between them. And there went out a champion out of the camp of the Philistines, named Goliath, of Gath, whose height was six cubits and a span.*
>
> *And he had an helmet of brass upon his head, and he was armed with a coat of mail; and the weight of the coat was five thousand shekels of brass. And he*

had greaves of brass upon his legs, and a target of brass between his shoulders. And the staff of his spear was like a weaver's beam; and his spear's head weighed six hundred shekels of iron: and one bearing a shield went before him.

And he stood and cried unto the armies of Israel, and said unto them, Why are ye come out to set your battle in array? am not I a Philistine, and ye servants to Saul? choose you a man for you, and let him come down to me. If he be able to fight with me, and to kill me, then will we be your servants: but if I prevail against him, and kill him, then shall ye be our servants, and serve us. And the Philistine said, I defy the armies of Israel this day; give me a man, that we may fight together. When Saul and all Israel heard those words of the Philistine, they were dismayed, and greatly afraid.

Verse 26 *And David spake to the men that stood by him, saying, What shall be done to the man that killeth this Philistine, and taketh away the reproach from Israel? for who is this uncircumcised Philistine, that he should defy the armies of the living God?*

David was the only person who felt that he could defeat Goliath. Everyone else was scared, insecure, and fearful. The scripture describes them, including Saul, as terrified and deeply shaken. Even though he was still positioned as king, Saul was not confident in his armor, stature, authority, or his ability to judge and overthrow Goliath. He was insecure in his spiritual and natural armor, and did not believe he was equipped to defeat Goliath. Had David fought with that armor, he would have been fighting through the well of fear, insecurity, terror, and defeat, as all of this was enmeshed in Saul's armor. You are only as strong as the armor you put on. This is why we are told to put on the armor of the Lord as that is the best and most complete armor we can wear (***Ephesians 6:11-12***).

At this point of fighting Goliath, God had already rejected Saul and David was anointed as the new king.

> *1Samuel 13:13-14 And Samuel said to Saul, Thou hast done foolishly: thou hast not kept the commandment of the LORD thy God, which he commanded thee: for now would the LORD have established thy kingdom upon Israel for ever. But now thy kingdom shall not continue:*
> *the LORD hath sought him a man after his own heart, and the LORD hath commanded him to be captain over his people, because thou hast not kept that which the LORD commanded thee.*

> *1Samuel 16:1 And the LORD said unto Samuel, How long wilt thou mourn for Saul, seeing I have rejected him from reigning over Israel? fill thine horn with oil, and go, I will send thee to Jesse the Bethlehemite: for I have provided me a king among his sons.*

> **Verse 11-13** *And Samuel said unto Jesse, Are here all thy children? And he said, There remaineth yet the youngest, and, behold, he keepeth the sheep. And Samuel said unto Jesse, Send and fetch him: for we will not sit down till he come hither. And he sent, and brought him in. Now he was ruddy, and withal of a beautiful countenance, and goodly to look to. And the Lord said, Arise, anoint him: for this is he. Then Samuel took the horn of oil, and anointed him in the midst of his brethren: and the Spirit of the Lord came upon David from that day forward. So Samuel rose up, and went to Ramah.*

Had David fought with Saul's armor, he would have been fighting through the judgement of Saul and fighting with rejected armor. He would have went out to fight in the name of the Lord, but God would not have shown up. God had left Saul. David would have been fighting confused, as how can the accepted king fight under the covering of the rejected king???? This is the reason David fought in the name of the Lord. He was not fighting under Saul as Saul was rejected, but under the covering of the Lord who had all authority over him and who he was as king.

> **1Samuel 17:45** *Then said David to the Philistine, Thou comest to me with a sword, and with a spear, and with a shield: but I come to thee in the name of the Lord of hosts, the God of the armies of Israel, whom thou hast defied.*

Aside from David's brothers, the people were not aware of what had transpired in secret, and that Saul was no longer the king and the leader of the people in the Lord's eyes. Therefore, when Goliath, the regional principality, came to war against Israel, Saul did not have the authority to defeat him. Saul no longer had any authority in that region nor in the spirit realm. Had David fought with Saul's armor, he would have had no authority as God had already judged Saul, rejected him and stripped him of his armor and stature.

David would have been coming under the succession of Saul if he would have worn Saul's armor. This would have been out of order as David was not called to succeed Saul. He was called to replace him and to bring the kingdom of Israel back in alignment with God.

Because our dance styles (mantles) are different, it is important to seek God about what we are to wear, what our armor is to look like, and seek to find garments, or have garments created that represent our purpose and calling.

We also need to take into consideration that though people wear beautiful garments, they may not have the relationship with God conducive to that garment. They may be in position, but be rejected, judged, lack the authority, maturity, blessings, and stature of walking in the armor and authority that is upon their life. We should therefore, cease from borrowing and wearing what others wear. Make the financial sacrifices to purchase your own garments, while seeking God for the designs that are conducive to your body type, authority, stature, and that speaks to the dance mantle that is upon your life.

SPIRIT OF THE COPYCAT AS IT RELATES TO DANCE STYLES

In *1Samuel 17:38-40*, we have David preparing to fight Goliath and Saul attempting to dress David in his armor.

> *And Saul armed David with his armour, and he put an helmet of brass upon his head; also he armed him with a coat of mail. And David girded his sword upon his armour, and he assayed to go; for he had not proved it. And David said unto Saul, I cannot go with these; for I have not proved them. And David put them off him. And he took his staff in his hand, and chose him five smooth stones out of the brook, and put them in a shepherd's bag which he had, even in a scrip; and his sling was in his hand: and he drew near to the Philistine.*

Because David was in King Saul's palace, he could have taken this opportunity to come under the king's warrior anointing, especially when Saul offered his armor to him. Even though it would have been honorable to wear the king's armor, David lets Saul know that he could not wear his armor because he had not proved it. Essentially David was saying that he was not used to the armor - that though it was powerful, it was not for him. David then took a staff in his hand, a sling, and put five smooth stones in a bag. This did not seem like suitable armor to fight a giant - a principality. However, David was familiar with this armor and knew how to wear and operate the armor to bring about success and breakthrough.

Armor symbolizes a person's garment, mantle, arsenal of weaponry, stature and authority to judge and govern people, atmospheres, regions and demons.

> ***Ephesians 6:11-12*** *Put on the whole armour of God, that ye may be able to stand against the wiles of the devil. For we wrestle not against flesh and blood, but against principalities, against powers, against the rulers of the darkness of this world, against spiritual wickedness in high places.*

Though others did not know the power of David's armor, he knew it. He knew that he was capable of killing that which was as powerful as a bear and a lion, which would be comparable to Goliath in the animal kingdom.

> ***1Samuel 17:32-37*** *And David said to Saul, Let no man's heart fail because of him; thy servant will go and fight with this Philistine. And Saul said to David, Thou art not able to go against this Philistine to fight with him: for thou art but a youth, and he a man of war from his youth. And David said unto Saul, Thy servant kept his father's sheep, and there came a lion, and a bear, and took a lamb out of the flock: And I went out after him, and smote him, and delivered it out of his mouth: and when he arose against me, I caught him by his beard, and smote him, and slew him. Thy servant slew both the lion and the bear: and this uncircumcised Philistine shall be as one of them,*

> *seeing he hath defied the armies of the living God. David said moreover, The Lord that delivered me out of the paw of the lion, and out of the paw of the bear, he will deliver me out of the hand of this Philistine. And Saul said unto David, Go, and the Lord be with thee.*

Many dancers will come under dance leaders and teams for training and mentoring, and will end up wearing that leader's armor while rejecting or negating, the armor upon their lives. Many dancers will resort to becoming copycats of their leaders, rather than originals of their own dance anointing. Many will not know how to cultivate their own style of movement, or will not seek the Holy Spirit on how to cultivate their own style of movement, which results in untapped potential and anointing, while becoming a counterfeit of the ministry's culture.

Sometimes some dance leaders sculpt members into becoming mimics of themselves, rather than cultivating the personal anointing that is on members, so they can come into the mantle of dance that is on their lives. This results in Christian dance becoming a common fad where all our dances and movements look alike, as originality and uniqueness is stolen and annihilated.

Some dance leaders make ministers feel inadequate and inferior for being different. The dance leader is not sensitive to the call and purpose that is upon that minister's life so they thwart the anointing, rather than empower the anointing and creativity of God that is on that minister's life. Some dance leaders do not recognize that the creativity and anointing of each member, empowers the team to defeat the wiles of the enemy. Though all soldiers in the army are trained the same, each one of them have unique personalities, giftings, duties, and purposes that are essential to defeating the enemy, while conquering land, and territory. When we strip a dance minister of their armor, we strip the ministry of a key weapon that is essential to overthrowing the enemy and establishing the kingdom in the earth.

In the world, copycats are none as "*clones.*" It is not cool to be a "*clone*" in the world as this means you are an imitation of the real thing. The world also tends to reject anything that rejects originality when it comes to the arts. God considers clones to be idols. God hates idolatry because it dilutes, steals, kills, and destroys his authenticity in people. He is not allowed to be uniquely and authentically represented in that person.

> ***Exodus 20:3-4*** *Thou shalt have no other gods before me. Thou shalt not make unto thee any graven image, or any likeness of any thing that is in heaven above, or that is in the earth beneath, or that is in the water under the earth.*

> ***Leviticus 26:1*** *Ye shall make you no idols nor graven image, neither rear you up a standing image, neither shall ye set up [any] image of stone in your land, to bow down unto it: for I [am] the LORD your God.*

When you become a copycat of someone else, you have not only become a clone, but an idol. If you clone others to be like you, you have actually formed (carved and shaped) an idol. And though you think you are ministering unto the Lord, you are actually ministering to your idol. The idol carving of someone else or of your own self.

> **2Timothy 3:1-3** *This know also, that in the last days perilous times shall come. For men shall be lovers of their own selves, covetous, boasters, proud, blasphemers, disobedient to parents, unthankful, unholy, Without natural affection, trucebreakers, false accusers, incontinent, fierce, despisers of those that are good, Traitors, heady, highminded, lovers of pleasures more than lovers of God; Having a form of godliness, but denying the power thereof: from such turn away.*

David was confident that God would deliver him, therefore, he was not concerned whether his armor was sufficient. Often we copy other peoples' dance styles because we think that is the determinant for bringing deliverance and breakthrough to those we are ministering too. If you do not have the anointing, favor, blessing, and authority to go with that dance style, you are just ministering movements. People will be blessed but lives will not be changed, and the enemy you were meant to conquer, remains in position of the conqueror. You went to war, but you did not win the fight. You were no challenge to the enemy because you were dancing under the grace of another person.

If you have lost your uniqueness and creativity due to copying someone else's dance style, repent and ask God to restore your mantle and identity as a dance minister.

If you are a dance leader that has cultivated a group of clones, repent and ask God to show you the mantle, purpose and calling of each member, how to train them under the anointing that is on your life and on the ministry, while helping to cultivate who each minister is personally and as a team member.

Today we apply the blood of Jesus to cleanse and break free from any spiritual armor that we have on that is not God's original armor for our lives. Today we embrace our unique dance giftings and get before God so that the Holy Spirit can teach us how to operate in the armor that is upon our lives. #SHIFT

SPIRITS USING DANCE TEAMS TO ATTACK ONE ANOTHER

When David was dancing before the ark of the Lord in *2Samuel 6:14-21*, he was dancing with all his might in a linen ephod that was more like his undergarments than his kingly apparel. His wife looked out from a window and was appalled by what he was wearing. She then rebuked and mocked him when he came home and ridiculed his dance as if it was perversion.

> *Verse 14-21 And David danced before the Lord with all his might; and David was girded with a linen ephod. So David and all the house of Israel brought up the ark of the Lord with shouting, and with the sound of the trumpet. And as the ark of the Lord came into the city of David, Michal Saul's daughter looked through a window, and saw king David leaping and dancing before the Lord; and she despised him in her heart. And they brought in the ark of the Lord, and set it in his place, in the midst of the tabernacle that David had pitched for it: and David offered burnt offerings and peace offerings before the Lord.*
>
> *And as soon as David had made an end of offering burnt offerings and peace offerings, he blessed the people in the name of the Lord of hosts. And he dealt among all the people, even among the whole multitude of Israel, as well to the women as men, to every one a cake of bread, and a good piece of flesh, and a flagon of wine. So all the people departed every one to his house. Then David returned to*

> *bless his household. And Michal the daughter of Saul came out to meet David, and said, How glorious was the king of Israel to day, who uncovered himself to day in the eyes of the handmaids of his servants, as one of the vain fellows shamelessly uncovereth himself! And David said unto Michal, It was before the Lord, which chose me before thy father, and before all his house, to appoint me ruler over the people of the Lord, over Israel: therefore will I play before the Lord.*

Often dance members and teams will do this to one another. Instead of respecting, teaching, and empowering one another, a spirit of judgement, self-righteousness, and ridicule unleashes as dance ministers and dance teams go forth in their dance ministry. People will be ridiculed for not wearing appropriate garments or apparel that the judging person feels is suitable attire. Although at times this may be true, the word curses that are released through self-righteous judgment causes spirits of comparison and competition to rule the atmosphere of interactions. Those that need to come into a knowing in this area end up being offended, ostracized and hurt rather than drawn into unity and knowledge, such that they are taught appropriate dance attire and ministry etiquette as it relates to dance and dance ministry.

Rather than belittling others who may not be ministering in the appropriate garments, befriend them, learn their maturity level regarding garments and the ministry of dance, and seek God for revelation on how to empower them in these areas.

Remember the enemy wants dance ministers and dance ministries to be divided and in competition. He wants the world's attributes, perceptions and perversions to rule our ministries so churches and people will reject them. He knows the power of our calling and giftings, since he himself was an arts minister for heaven.

> ***Ezekiel 28:13*** *Thou hast been in Eden the garden of God; every precious stone was thy covering, the sardius, topaz, and the diamond, the beryl, the onyx, and the jasper, the sapphire, the emerald, and the carbuncle, and gold: the workmanship of thy tabrets and of thy pipes was prepared in thee in the day that thou wast created.*

We must band together so he will not use us against one another, where he just sit back and watch as we take one another out with our judgmental words and vain righteousness.

MOCKING & PERVERSE SPIRITS THAT DEFAME DANCE MINISTRY

In *2Samuel 6:14-20*, we find David being attacked by a mocking spirit through his wife for dancing naked before the ark of the Lord. This spirit mocked his worship and dance ministry unto the Lord, and attempted to make him feel as if it was disrespectful, degrading, worthless and perverse. Her efforts to curse him and his dance ministry with her negative words, became a curse upon her womb and her ability to reproduce as in *Verse 23* the scripture states that she had no children unto death.

> *Verse 20-23* *Then David returned to bless his household. And Michal the daughter of Saul came out to meet David, and said, How glorious was the king of Israel to day, who uncovered himself to day in the eyes of the handmaids of his servants, as one of the vain fellows shamelessly uncovereth himself! And David said unto Michal, It was before the Lord, which chose me before thy father, and before all his house, to appoint me ruler over the people of the Lord, over Israel: therefore will I play before the Lord. And I will yet be more vile than thus, and will be base in mine own sight: and of the maidservants which thou hast spoken of, of them shall I be had in honour. Therefore Michal the daughter of Saul had no child unto the day of her death.*

This mocking spirit is actually rooted in religion. The mocking spirit strives to kill the dance minister and dance ministries, while keeping dance from being an avenue of worship and weapon against the enemy within a region. Within a church, the same thing applies. Churches are rooted in a community to be a change agent and avenue for resources and transformation. Churches should also dispel principalities and powers in the community while bringing in God's presence. So just like David danced in the city, when you dance in a church, you are combating principalities and powers in that community.

> *1Samuel 6:16-17 And as the ark of the Lord came into the city of David, Michal Saul's daughter looked through a window, and saw king David leaping and dancing before the Lord; and she despised him in her heart. And they brought in the ark of the Lord, and set it in his place, in the midst of the tabernacle that David had pitched for it: and David offered burnt offerings and peace offerings before the Lord.*

David was ministering a spiritual work of establishing the presence of God in that city. The enemy wanted him to be focused on the way he may have come across to the people. But David was more concerned about whether God was pleased and received glory.

Mocking spirits tend to approach a dancer or team right after a mighty move of God. They will begin to question the ministry that went forth, its purpose, and the name and glory of God. Often they seek to have you defending what you ministered and even defending ministers on your team. If another dance minister or team ministered, they will come to you in effort to get you to speak ill of that minister or ministry. Their purpose is to divide, mock and defame dance ministers and dance ministries and prove that these ministries should not be in the church.

We must learn to recognize the mocking spirits of religion that are sent to defame and kill dance ministers and ministries. We must not let them intimidate us into sitting on our gifting and calling. We must cease from allowing them to speak perversion over us and into the ministry of dance. David protested to be even more abase than he was in his dance ministry and worship unto the Lord. Do the same and allow your ministry to shut the mouth and womb of this mocking spirit of religion from breeding other religious mockers into your life, team or the ministry of fellow dance ministers.

> **Verse 22-23** *And I will yet be more vile than thus, and will be base in mine own sight: and of the maidservants which thou hast spoken of, of them shall I be had in honour. Therefore Michal the daughter of Saul had no child unto the day of her death.*

When you put the mocking spirit in its place, it will kill its ability to reproduce in other people and the church. The spirit will have no offspring where by it plants, produces, and reproduces seeds of strife, ridicule, and death. This does not have to be done in a disrespectful or angry manner. Ask God to guide your words, and if he leads you to speak, share in a respectful confident manner. God may also have you combat this spirit in prayer rather than deal with it head on. The main key is not to agree with what this spirit is saying and take their words as truth as then you come into agreement with it. And since this is an aborting spirit, you are coming into agreement with the spirit of death.

Also David was confident, focused on his assignment and God receiving glory. He was willing to sacrifice self so that God could be glorified. When we are in churches or among ministries where dance ministry has not been fully received, we must be more focused on our assignment to that ministry and to God, and must be willing to sacrifice ourselves to see God's presence established in that church or regarding that assignment. David was making sure he brought the ark up to the tabernacle in Israel in a way that pleased God. So he did not care who did not like his abandonment, humility, and honor before the Lord. He did not even care what his wife thought about him. We have to want God's approval more than the peoples' approval. Otherwise the mocking spirit of religion will have us inferior about our calling and the assignment God has granted to our hands.

SPIRITS OF AFFLICTION THAT ATTACK DANCE MINISTERS

Dance minister and ministries tend to experience much affliction by people and demons. Although we can bring afflictions upon ourselves, many of these afflictions are due to the calling and purpose upon our lives.

> *Psalms 34:17-20 The righteous cry, and the Lord heareth and delivereth them out of all their troubles. The Lord is nigh unto them that are of a broken heart; and saveth such as be of a contrite spirit. Many are the afflictions of the righteous: but the Lord delivereth him out of them all. He keepeth all his bones: not one of them is broken.*

<u>Afflictions</u> in the Hebrew is *"ra"* and means:
1. bad, natural or more evil, adversity, tightened (tight spots), calamity
2. distress, sorry, great grief, trouble, wickedness
3. adversity, wretchedness, wrong doing, persecution, tribulation
4. mischief, hurt, ill (favor), displeasure, soreness, noisome

The minute you start praising and worshipping God, while declaring his name, goodness, power, authority, kingdom, in the earth, you have entered a fight with the devil whether you acknowledge it or not.

> *Psalms 149:6-9 Let the high praises of God be in their mouth, and a twoedged sword in their hand;*

> *To execute vengeance upon the heathen, and punishments upon the people; To bind their kings with chains, and their nobles with fetters of iron; To execute upon them the judgment written: this honour have all his saints. Praise ye the Lord.*

Uhmmmm…..High praise insinuates an uprising. When there is an uprising, something is being stirred up and confronted, and contended for. If you are causing an uprising with your prayer and worship, and if you are executing vengeance, punishing, binding, executing judgment, then uhmmmm, you must have an enemy and you must be at war with something or someone.

> **Psalms 150** *Praise ye the Lord. Praise God in his sanctuary: praise him in the firmament of his power. Praise him for his mighty acts: praise him according to his excellent greatness. Praise him with the sound of the trumpet: praise him with the psaltery and harp. Praise him with the timbrel and dance: praise him with stringed instruments and organs. Praise him upon the loud cymbals: praise him upon the high sounding cymbals. Let every thing that hath breath praise the Lord. Praise ye the Lord.*

<u>Praise</u> is *Halal* in the Hebrew and means:
1. to shine (fig. of God's favor), to flash forth light
2. to praise, boast, be boastful, boastful ones, boasters, make a boast
3. to be praised, be made praiseworthy, be commended, be worthy of praise

4. glory, make one's boast, to make a fool of, make into a fool
5. to act madly, act like a madman

When we boast about God, it makes the devil and wicked people angry and releases a rage of retaliation. Especially when we sacrifice our entire beings to give him praise and worship, and when our praise and worship is overthrowing or has the potential to overthrow demonic kingdoms.

Seeming this is the lifestyle and purpose of a dance minister and dance ministry, the enemy will send constant attacks to distract, weary, persecute, and overthrow the dance minister and team. He wants us in distress, great sorrow and grief, closed in, closed minded, cornered, restless, irritated, in drama and confusion, where we cannot hear God or be used by God. Sometime these afflictions attack the dance minister or team for no apparent reason at all. You just wake up grieved, sorrow of heart and soul, and do not know why. Persecution and drama seem to find you and you have no clue what is brought it about. Family attacks you. People on your job attacks you. And more than anything, the church body attacks you. These are the very people who are benefiting from your ministry, yet they are open doors for the enemy to afflict you. This is the reason David said *"many are the afflictions."* David understood that the attacks could come from anywhere at any time, and that he did not have to do anything to cause the afflictions.

> **Psalms 132:1** *Lord, remember David, and all his afflictions.*
>
> **The Amplified Bible** *LORD, [earnestly] remember to David's credit all his humiliations and hardships and endurance.*

<u>This word *afflictions* is "ana" in the Hebrew and means:</u>
1. the idea of looking down or downtrodden
2. literally to depress, oppress, or debase
3. weak, weakened, occupied or busy with affliction
4. to humble self, submit self

David had endured a lot and knew the power and blessing of humbling himself unto God even in his afflictions. He was asking God to remember him and if you read the rest of **Psalms 132**, you will notice that David was requesting God's to help and favor to fulfill his promise and assignment of bringing the ark of the Lord home to Israel.

Often when we are experiencing affliction, the last thing we do is humble ourselves unto God. Generally, we began combating the devil, while being angry at God that we continue to endure hardship and tribulation. Our well of expression tends to be pride and righteous indignation as we strive to tell God how much we sacrifice ourselves for his glory. Being exalted in pride and indignation allows the enemy to afflict us all the more. We are not in a place to hear God, and cannot discern that the enemy is afflicting to steal our focus so we do not fulfill the assignment at hand.

As dance ministers, it is important that we live and abide in a submitted and honored posture of praise and worship, especially when we are enduring afflictions. This positions fortifies us against the enemy, where we cannot be overcome by the many troubles and attacks. Let's explore the benefits of praise and worship as a lifestyle by focusing on the language being used in the Psalms 150 scriptural passage:

1. Praise ye the Lord - The scripture begins by giving us a command to praise the Lord. We are commanded to remain in this place of consistent and continual exalted praise unto the Lord. He is receiving glory no matter what is occurring in our lives.

2. Praise God in his sanctuary - Praise positions us inside of the sanctuary of God. *Sanctuary* in the Strong's in this scripture means *"apartness, holiness, separateness, of God, of places, of things."* As we praise, we are being separated from the afflictions and troubles, and drawn into the holiness and consecration of God in His sanctuary.

3. Praise him in the firmament of his power - *Firmament* in the Strong's for this scripture means *"extended surface, vault of heaven supporting waters above, solid and supporting waters from above."* *Vault* in dictionary.com means an *"arched structure,*

usually made up of stones, concrete, or bricks forming a ceiling or roof over a hall or room, a strong metal cabinet, usually fireproof and burglarproof, for storage and safekeeping of valuables." Praise brings you into a place safety while being fortified and vaulted in God's power where nothing can be stolen or destroyed.

4. Praise him for his mighty acts, Praise him according to his excellent greatness - As you praise, you are shifted into focusing on the mighty deeds and acts of God. This makes the affliction null and void as you are flooded with the multitude and abundance of God's goodness, glory, might, strength, valor, and bravery.

5. Praise him with the sound of the trumpet: praise him with the psaltery and harp. Praise him with the timbrel and dance, praise him with stringed instruments and organs. Praise him upon the loud cymbals: praise him upon the high sounding cymbals - Your atmosphere begins to be overtaken by the sound, authority, and expression that shifts your life and situations into alignment with the Lord. Blasting sounds and judging movements are released to thwart the sounds and attacks of the enemy. Praise becomes the very essence of the atmosphere around you, and through acts of praise and worship, God's glory, power, and authority are actively ignited, stirred, and established on your behalf.

6. Let every thing that hath breath praise the Lord. Praise ye the Lord! - Praise is a place that you live from. You use your very breath to praise the Lord as it is your divine inspiration. It becomes a place that you reside in and operate through.

Psalms 91:1-4 He that dwelleth in the secret place of the most High
shall abide under the shadow of the Almghty. I will say of the Lord, He is my refuge and my fortress; my God; in him will I trust. Surely he shall deliver thee from the snare of the fowler, and from the noisome pestilence. He shall cover thee with his feathers, and under his wings shalt thou trust: his truth shall be thy shield and buckler.

2Timothy 2:3-4 Thou therefore endure hardness, as a good soldier of Jesus Christ. No man that warreth entangleth himself with the affairs of this life; that he may please him who hath chosen him to be a soldier.

Accept the fullness of afflictions being a part of your calling today. **SHIFT!**

SICKNESS & INFIRMITY THAT ATTACK DANCE MINISTERS

Because our bodies are avenues to which God uses us to minister, dance ministers are often attacked by spirits of sickness and infirmity. Some dance ministers deal with constant or prolonged sicknesses and infirmities. Sometimes this occurs if there are generational curses of sickness and infirmity that have ruled the family line. The enemy will use this avenue to continually wreak havoc on the dancer so that they are discouraged, distracted or limited and hindered in their movement. And sometimes these attacks due to the calling of the dance minister. The body is being attacked because it is the very instrument being used for God's glory.

One of the greatest powers of a dance minister is the ability to manifest the presence of the Lord. Where the spirit of the Lord is, there is liberty *(2Corinthians 3:17)*. The enemy does not want the dance minister liberated to minister, and he does not want the people liberated to receive of the presence of God.

As a dance minister, I am constantly battling spirits of sickness and infirmity, and spirits of incurable disease. I dread going to the doctor as often times what I am battling, has no cure. Over the years, I have learned that these spirits attack in effort to distract, bind, oppress, frustrate, torment, disempower, condemn, and shame the dance minister. Sometimes these spirits attack to send the dancer on a wild goose chase of trying to receive healing from personal issues where really there is no basis for the illness or affliction.

> **1Peter 5:7-11** *Casting all your care upon him; for he careth for you.*
> *Be sober, be vigilant; because your adversary the devil, as a roaring lion, walketh about, seeking whom he may devour: Whom resist stedfast in the faith, knowing that the same afflictions are accomplished in your brethren that are in the world. But the God of all grace, who hath called us unto his eternal glory by Christ Jesus, after that ye have suffered a while, make you perfect, stablish, strengthen, settle you. To him be glory and dominion for ever and ever. Amen.*

Care in the Greek is *Merimna* and means "anxiety, distraction, solicitude (concern or anxiously desire)."

Sober means *"to be calm and collected in the spirit."* *Vigilant* means *"to be watchful and at strict attention."* The enemy walks around plotting ways to devours us. He sends distractions or uses our concerns to cause distraction and anxiety. And because we have SHIFTED from being cool, calm, and collected, to anxious, we have opened a door to the wiles of the enemy.

Devour means *"to eat, consume, destroy, swallow whole."* These attacks are meant to take us out so they hit us hard. But the word tells us that returning to a posture of steadfast faith is our best defense in these times. Our focus must be on understanding that the enemy is going to plot attacks against our bodies. We must stand in the unwavering truth of that the Lord is a deliverer and a healer, and even though we may suffer a while, God will restore us in his perfection, confirmation, strength, power, and sufficiency.

> ***The Amplified Bible*** *Casting the whole of your care [all your anxieties, all your worries, all your concerns, once and for all] on Him, for He cares for you affectionately and cares about you watchfully. Be well balanced (temperate, sober of mind), be vigilant and cautious at all times; for that enemy of yours, the devil, roams around like a lion roaring [in fierce hunger], seeking someone to seize upon and devour. Withstand him; be firm in faith [against his onset — rooted, established, strong, immovable, and determined], knowing that the same (identical) sufferings are appointed to your brotherhood (the whole body of Christians) throughout the world. And after you have suffered a little while, the God of all grace [Who imparts all blessing and favor], Who has called you to His [own] eternal glory in Christ Jesus, will Himself complete and make you what you ought to be, establish and ground you securely, and strengthen, and settle you. To Him be the dominion (power, authority, rule) forever and ever. Amen (so be it).*

SICKNESS THAT MANIFESTS AS WORDS OF KNOWLEDGE & REVELATION

Sometimes when a dance minister becomes afflicted or sick in their bodies or even multiple team members become oppressed with different types of ailments, God could be using this to reveal words of knowledge or revelation of what is going on in the people, church or organization, land, atmosphere or region to which you are ministering in. This is the reason it is important to know how the gifts of the Holy Spirit found in **1Corinthians 12:4-11** operate. Dancers are embodiments of the Holy Spirit. We can flow in and out of any gift of the Spirit at any given time.

> **1Corinthians 6:19** *What? know ye not that your body is the temple of the Holy Ghost which is in you, which ye have of God, and ye are not your own?*

There have been instances where my back will go out as I am preparing for an engagement or I will have different pains in my body. Or instances where my team members and I will experience similar ailments such as headaches, stomach problems, back pains, respiratory issues, bindings around the head or weightiness to name a few. Generally, when a dancer is ill, the first inclination is to cancel the ministry engagement. But my team and I have learned the importance of searching out these sicknesses, and discerning whether they are manifestations related to the ministry engagement.

Often when praying into these aliments, we will learn various oppressions that the people, land, atmosphere, or region is experiencing. When praying concerning these ailments, they will release, as we break their powers and strongholds off of people.

There are also instances that though we may war and intercede as God leads, these ailments will not dissolve until we go forth in ministering the word and will of God through the dance. It is however, important to have this revelation, for doing so makes us more offensive in our ability to dismantle the wiles of the enemy. This also provides greater purpose for the reason God is sending us to minister.

> ***1Corinthians 12:4-11*** *Now there are diversities of gifts, but the same Spirit. And there are differences of administrations, but the same Lord. And there are diversities of operations, but it is the same God which worketh all in all. But the manifestation of the Spirit is given to every man to profit withal. For to one is given by the Spirit the word of wisdom; to another the word of knowledge by the same Spirit; -- To another faith by the same Spirit; to another the gifts of healing by the same Spirit; -- To another the working of miracles; to another prophecy; to another discerning of spirits; to another divers kinds of tongues; to another the interpretation of tongues: But all these worketh that one and the selfsame Spirit, dividing to every man severally as he will.*

KINGDOM VISION FOR DANCE MINISTRIES

Often when it comes to the arts, members and affiliates are connected due to similar giftings, creativity, and peculiarity. Those involved are focused on displaying gifts, gaining recognition, building platforms, and advancing in the business. However, the ministry of dance is not a place for showcasing your talent, receiving validation, or fashioning your own kingdom. Dance ministry is liken to an army so there has to be commitment to God, one to another and to the vision. If there is no trust in God, one to another or in the vision off the battlefield, then there can be no sufficient trust to God, one to another, and in the vision when you are on the battlefield. When you minister for the Lord, there is divine purpose, so your connection is rooted in relationship and covenant. The dance minister recognizes that they have an obligation to God and to the ministry. Walking in their calling and fulfilling every kingdom assignment is their focus and goal. A dance minister must have vision to fulfill such a mission. When they have vision, the dance minister is not quick to leave when:
- Things do not go their way
- The ministry is in a time of pressing, plowing, and/or warfare
- They are corrected or made accountable in their character and actions
- They get bored or the honeymoon phase of ministry has passed

- The ministry assignments out ways the need for recognition, validation and fame
- The sacrifice to minister for God costs them their entire lives

Dance ministers should:
- Have a covenant with God and have an understanding of the vision of dance ministry on their lives
- Have a covenant relationship with dance ministers that they are on a team with or who they are in fellowship with
- Have a understanding and covenant relationship with the vision plan of the ministry team they are assigned to

Covenant is a formal or informal agreement, promise, and vow of commitment to fulfill specified duties and assignments that God is requiring of you concerning your life, calling, ministry of dance, and the vision of the dance ministry you belong to. Often people make informal vows, but do not keep them. It tends to be words spoken in a time of excitement and passion, with no vision as to what lies ahead, what God is saying or requiring, and what it will take to fulfill that vow. Also many dance ministers and teams do not have written visions concerning the purpose for their ministry; therefore when these vows are made, there is little clarity and sight for the vision of dance ministry and the reason God birthed it in the earth. The challenge with this is whether written or spoken, God holds us accountable to any covenant we make. If we tell God we will be his minister of dance and if we agree to be a part of a dance team, we are responsible for seeking him for vision so we can have the revelation, knowledge and tools needed to complete our covenant assignment.

> ***Deuteronomy 23:21-23*** *When you make a vow to the LORD your God, you shall not delay to pay it, for it would be sin in you, and the LORD your God will surely require it of you. "However, if you refrain from vowing, it would not be sin in you. "You shall be careful to perform what goes out from your lips, just as you have voluntarily vowed to the LORD your God, what you have promised.*

> ***Matthew 30:20*** *If a man makes a vow to the LORD, or takes an oath to bind himself with a binding obligation, he shall not violate his word; he shall do according to all that proceeds out of his mouth.*

In order to keep covenant, people must have vision. Vision empowers the dance minister to be accountable:
- to the calling that is on their life
- the people they are in ministry with
- and to what God is speaking regarding them helping to bring the vision of that ministry to pass

Proverbs 29:18 *Where there is no vision, the people perish: but he that keepeth the law, happy is he.*

Perish is Para in the Hebrew and means:
1. avenge, avoid, bare, go back, make naked, perish

2. to loosen, by implication, to expose, dismiss; figuratively, absolve, begin
3. set at nought, refuse, uncover

When there is vision there is power! When there is vision there is power of:
- Sight & Clarity
- Enlightenment & Understanding
- Revelation
- Knowledge
- Prophecy
- Vivid Credibility
- Guidance
- Responsibility
- Accountability
- A Value of Honor, Character & Integrity
- Ideas & Creativity
- A Notion to Act & Follow Through
- A Focus
- A Clear Tangible Success Point
- Measure of Growth & Success
- Anticipation
- Potential & Opportunity
- Continual Growth, Elevation & Promotion
- A Press to Fulfill the Vision
- A Great Drive for Consistency
- Destiny Moments of Achievements & Rewards
- Supernatural Powers & Abilities to Carry & Sustain in the Vision
- Blessings, Favor, Divine Connections & Interventions
- Successorship & Generational Inheritance

When there is no vision there is no power. When there is no vision there is
- Blindness
- Sightlessness
- No Expected End
- Little to No Hope
- Little to No Progress
- Little to No Destiny Moments of Achievements & Rewards
- The Insanity of Restarting & Doing the Same Things Over & Over
- Cycling in Unfruitful Tasks & Endeavors
- Lack of Focus
- Lack of Growth, Elevation & Promotion
- Looseness
- Excuses
- Inconsistencies
- Value of Honor, Character & Integrity
- No Restraint/Lawlessness/Wild Behaviors
- Little to No Credibility
- Frustration & Confusion Regarding the Purpose & Success of the Vision
- Unnecessary Drama
- Unnecessary Warfare
- Stress, Mental Instabilities, & Physical Ailments due to Burnout
- Self & Demonic Sabotage
- Avoidance with Completing Tasks
- Potential to Use Role/Position in the Vision to Avenge, Retaliate, Wreak Havoc, Cause

Division, Control, Stagnate, Imprison or Kill the Vision
- Potential to Expose, Dismiss, Contaminate, Compromise, Hinder, or Negate the Vision
- Division, False or Erred Prophecy & Split Paths that are not the Direction or Plan of God
- Little to No Strength to Carry or Fight for the Vision
- Successorship & Generational Inheritance

Vision is so important because many dance ministers:
- Will start teams then when things become hard, they will quit and the ministry will not be adequately established in the earth realm.
- Become a part of a ministry, then will quit before they have completed their assignment or received the equipment they need to advance further in their ministry.
- Will be the only dancer in the church, but because they are the only one, they will not fulfill vows that they made to the Lord to birth, plant, and plow the ministry. They will have assignments of worship, intercession and warfare, but when God unctions them to minister, they will not go forth. They will sit on the pew with all types of excuses of the reason they cannot flow as God is leading.
- Go from church to church, dance ministry to dance ministry with little vision to help them be rooted and grounded in their call to dance.
- Join ministries for fad and form, but lack purpose.

- Attend dance ministry schools for connection, licensing, and prestige, while losing their identity, individuality and kingdom purpose.

As you seek God for vision of your dance ministry and team, write down what he shares with you.

> **Habakkuk 2:1-3** *I will stand upon my watch, and set me upon the tower, and will watch to see what he will say unto me, and what I shall answer when I am reproved. And the Lord answered me, and said, Write the vision, and make it plain upon tables, that he may run that readeth it. For the vision is yet for an appointed time, but at the end it shall speak, and not lie: though it tarry, wait for it; because it will surely come, it will not tarry.*

- Make sure your vision is clear and you understand your current assignment in each given season, even if you do not have the full revelation of how the vision will continually unfold.
- Make sure your vision is in alignment with the church you are under or with your ministry covering. If it does not seem to flow, make sure you understand the purpose of it and how it will connect in the future and how it will work together for the greater kingdom good.
- Make sure your vision includes the character, integrity, lifestyle, and consecration needed to fulfill the vision.
- Make sure each team member has a copy of the vision. Make sure they understand the

purpose of the vision and what you believe their personal role is in helping to fulfill the vision.
- Also encourage them to seek God for revelation concerning their part in helping to fulfill the vision. Have them submit this to you in writing or in an email.
- Revisit the vision at least once or twice a year and update it as God leads. Give each member a copy of the updated vision.
- When team members demonstrate a lax in the vision, refer them to their commitment to God in the vision and pray for them to be refocused, empowered and recommitted to what God told them to do.
- Have teams revisit the vision yearly. Give them ample time before the Lord in exploring the following questions, while submitting them to you in writing or email form.
  1. What has your spiritual progress and challenges have been like this past year?
  2. Did you keep covenant with God, while achieving your goals and what God desired of you personally and spiritually? Explain your progress or lack thereof in detail. What would you do differently? What would you do better?
  3. How did the ministry impact your growth and/or lack thereof?
  4. What is God saying for personally for the coming year?
  5. What is God saying for you as it relates to the ministry for this coming year? What is

he saying as it relates to your relationships with team members and to leadership?
6. What disciplines do you need to achieve your goals?
7. What do you desire and feel you need from the in order to achieve your goals?
8. What do you need from God to achieve your goals?
9. List three goals you are committed to working on to achieve the things God is requiring of you.
10. List three goals you are commuted to work on to grow in your gifts and callings.
11. Share anything else that would benefit what God is asking if you for this coming year and that would benefit the team in fulfilling the ministry vision.

- Pray for each team member and journal what God is speaking concerning the yearly exploration questions. Meet with each team member personally and explore what God shared with you and what God shared with them. Make sure they have clear vision for the upcoming year and how to remain in covenant with God, their dance ministry, and the vision of the dance team.

COVENANT IMPARTATIONS

In *1Samuel 17:38-40* we find Saul trying to give David his armor to wear for war, but David could not fit it. However in *1Samuel 18:1-6*, Jonathan, Saul's son, gives David his armor and it fits accordingly:

> *1Samuel 17:38-40 And Saul armed David with his armour, and he put an helmet of brass upon his head; also he armed him with a coat of mail. And David girded his sword upon his armour, and he assayed to go; for he had not proved it. And David said unto Saul, I cannot go with these; for I have not proved them. And David put them off him. And he took his staff in his hand, and chose him five smooth stones out of the brook, and put them in a shepherd's bag which he had, even in a scrip; and his sling was in his hand: and he drew near to the Philistine.*

> *1Samuel 18:1-6 And it came to pass, when he had made an end of speaking unto Saul, that the soul of Jonathan was knit with the soul of David, and Jonathan loved him as his own soul. And Saul took him that day, and would let him go no more home to his father's house. Then Jonathan and David made a covenant, because he loved him as his own soul. And Jonathan stripped himself of the robe that was upon him, and gave it to David, and his garments, even to his sword, and to his bow, and to his girdle. And David went out whithersoever Saul sent him, and behaved himself wisely: and Saul set him over the men of war, and he was accepted in the sight of*

> *all the people, and also in the sight of Saul's servants.*

Saul was striving to give David an impartation that was not in the right timing, order and plan of God, and that was not conducive to the anointing and character upon David's life. He also was striving to impart an intimate part of his anointing without relationship, divine connection, or spiritual commitment. Moreover, Saul was striving to impart his mantle from a place of trying to equip David for battle rather than from a place of recognizing he was already equipped. Saul was trying to make David like him rather than allowing David to be himself, and imparting into him from that perspective. These are some of the reasons Saul's armor did not fit David.

God, however, knitted the soul of Jonathan to the soul of David which established a loving covenant bond between the two of them. Jonathan also imparted his armor to David from a place of honor, love and respect of who David already was, rather than who he was trying to make David be. Therefore, when Jonathan stripped his armor and gave it to David, it fit him and as David behaved and wore it wisely (with respect, integrity, success, skill), and favor with the people and the King's servants followed his life.

A lot of times we want impartations or receive impartations from people but they may be imparting from a place of pride, stinginess, or misrepresentation of what they think we need, deserve or should have. These types of impartations may negate the anointing on our lives, or have to be force fitted to work with the anointing upon our lives. They do not fit, yet we are trying to make them be something that God has not designed. These impartations tend to be given with conditions or out of a present assignment or need, rather than being an impartation that can be sustained and empowered throughout our destiny lifestyle.

Saul sought to arm David which was an equipping for the moment. Jonathan stripped himself to impart into David. He poured himself, his life into David. Saul gave out of his surplus, Jonathan sacrificed himself. That is the foundation and essence of covenant.

Saul no longer allowed David to return to live with his father. David remained at the palace with Saul and Jonathan. Saul sought to become a spiritual parent to David, but because this was not his role in his life, he could only teach David a few things. And because of his own insecurity, he eventually became an enemy when David begin to flourish in his gifting and calling.

When we try to make people more than they should be or when people try to be more than they should be, it opens the door for contention and strife. Sometimes you become enemies due to one or both parties operating out of immature, insecure and/or unhealed wounds within the soul.

MATURITY IN YOUR GIFTING & CALLING

I want to address this topic because it is so essential to continuously cultivate our giftings and calling so that when we go forth in ministry we carry and deliver the word and message of God with quality, authority, boldness, and care. When we are not continually learning, we become relaxed and lazy in the vision for our lives, and for who and what God has granted to our hands. We also have a mindset that we can minister any type of way, while still being pleasing to God, and effective in delivering and healing people. **THIS IS A DECEPTION OF THE ENEMY! SHIFT!**

Although dance ministry is still an area of ministry that is not fully received, some of it is because of immaturity in handling our giftings and callings. In many ways the ministry has become its own demise because it has been treated more like a social club ministry for kids, youth, ostracized church members, or those seeking to fulfill their own identity issues and need for approval, rather than truly attempting to impact and transform people's lives. The best way to combat the social club spirit and identity complexes is by treating dance as ministry, while cultivating your giftings and callings, so you can be the example that others need in order to view and respect it as ministry. **SHIFT!**

Cultivating your dance ministry is not just about attending dance classes and dance conferences. It is essential to know the full calling on your life and begin to walk in it, rather than just hiding behind dance.

- WHO ARE YOU????
- WHAT IS YOUR CALLING AS A WHOLE?
- HOW DOES YOUR CALLING TIE INTO YOUR MINISTRY OF DANCE?

Also the more word and revelation we partake of, the more of God we can manifest. Cultivate your walk with God through prayer, studying your word, seeking God for revelation, consistent fasting and consecration, and connecting with people who desire to see the power of God operate in their lives.

These issues and more must be worked on with God in our personal lives, so that when we go forth in ministry the fruit, character, and nature of God manifests in our ministry.

David is our example of someone who lived a lifestyle of working his issues out in his private time with God, such that even when he danced naked or in what we would consider not of kingly conduct, his ministry was pure unto and before the Lord.

When David did not deal with his issues with God, he was exposed before the people, because he was a glory carrier. We see this with the situation with Bathsheba in *2Samuel 11*. Bathsheba was a married woman, yet David saw her bathing one day and decided he would have his way with her. When she became pregnant, David called her husband Uriah from war and tried to get him to sleep with his wife. However, he would not go to his home because his assignment of war was not finished. David therefore, had him put in the front of the battle to ensure his death. David did all this to cover up the fact that he had gotten Bathsheba pregnant.

> *2Samuel. 12:9-13 Wherefore hast thou despised the commandment of the Lord, to do evil in his sight? thou hast killed Uriah the Hittite with the sword, and hast taken his wife to be thy wife, and hast slain him with the sword of the children of Ammon. Now therefore the sword shall never depart from thine house; because thou hast despised me, and hast taken the wife of Uriah the Hittite to be thy wife. Thus saith the Lord, Behold, I will raise up evil against thee out of thine own house, and I will take thy wives before thine eyes, and give them unto thy neighbour, and he shall lie with thy wives in the sight of this sun. For thou didst it secretly: but I will do this thing before all Israel, and before the sun.*

The sun symbolized the glory light of God. Since David had sinned in secret, God was allowing the glory that was to protect him, expose him. He was allowing the glory to create a window into his secret life so that all of Israel could know his sin, and see the judgment of the Lord upon him.

If David would have repented, God would have dealt with him in secret, but because he was not repentive and even sought to cover up his acts, God exposed him and then brought war and division upon his household. David became relaxed in the vision for his life and used his position for personal gain and pleasure. It cost him dearly and even though he was a man after God's own heart, his children and his kingdom paid the consequences for his actions (read *2Samuel 12-24*).

KINGDOM NUGGETS FOR DANCE MINISTERS & MINISTRIES

CULTIVATING THE TEAM
It is important that as dance ministers and ministries, we cultivate a culture of deliverance, healing and breakthrough. We must also cultivate an openness to receiving of these benefits of salvation continually, such that within ourselves we do not give room to the devil to infiltrate our lives and ministries. This also enables us to minister with power such that signs and wonder manifests in our midst.

> *Matthew 10:8* lepers, raise the dead, cast out devils: freely ye have received, freely give.

The leader is responsible for making sure this culture is active and consistent. The team should be equipped, trained, and cultivated in the ministry of deliverance, and be open to receiving healing and deliverance prayer from team members. The ministry of healing and deliverance should be a part of the nature and foundations of the dance ministry, as it is an important aspect of the completeness of the ministry. The team should know that they are not just dancers but ministers, and that deliverance and healing are a part of the lifestyle of being in God, and a part of the lifestyle of a minister.

It is important that we understand that as a dance ministry, practices are not just practice, and they are not just for the purpose of dancing. Because we are ministers we are preparing to release God's word and will through dance, and there will be things that will be sent to attack and hinder the word and the will of God from going forth. It is essential that we are aware of this and fortify ourselves and our teams accordingly.

To unveil such fortification, practices should include more than just dancing and choreography. They should also include:

- Intense times of prayer - for the team, atmosphere, region that you are in and the region that you will be ministering in, the people that you will be ministering to, and to cover you and your team from all attacks.
- Deliverance and healing (such that we ourselves are not an open door to the enemy; every member of the team is actively receiving deliverance and healing in their inner man, and growing in the nature, character, and wholeness of God).
- Searching God - spending time hearing from Him for His word, insight, and strategies on how to overcome spirits that may attack.
- Soaking in God's Presence – Spending time resting, and refreshing in God for the purposes of being filled, empowered, strengthened and renewed.

BE IN TUNE ATMOSPHERICALLY

As a leader and a team member it is necessary to be in tuned atmospherically where you are be able to discern and see what type of affliction, stronghold, oppression, or possession, the enemy may be releasing in the atmosphere of your practices and engagements. These attack may be sent against you, those you are ministering to or the region you are ministering in. You can discern what type of bondage is occurring by searching out the atmosphere before the beginning of your practices and before ministering at an engagement.

It is beneficial to come to practice and engagements early and search out the atmosphere such that you can already have revelation of the enemy's plots and plans, and you can take care of these attacks before practice starts and before you go forth in ministry. As the leader and the team becomes trained in this area, it becomes a part of your personal nature and the nature of the team. Eventually you will no longer have to remind yourself or encourage your team to search out the atmosphere, as it will be a part of their dance ministry lifestyle.

When searching out an atmosphere you can begin by asking God:
- What is present in the people, building, room, and region you are practicing or ministering in
- To show you or speak to you regarding the principalities, powers, bondages, etc. that may be in the atmosphere or region
- To reveal what that which is has been planted to attack and serve as a hindrance to you and your team

As God reveals these things to you ask him for

strategy to overcome them. Also ask him what the atmosphere needs to be conducive to the team having an effective practice, or an effective ministry engagement. After you receive insight and strategies, gather your team together and share what God revealed to you. Take the time to pray against what is revealed.

It is important each time your team gathers to practice or to minister at an engagement that you all pray before beginning to practice and before you minister. This places you all in an offensive stance to thwart the attacks of the enemy. You also immediately line up with God and come under His covering and protection, while being filled with his power and authority.

BE IN TUNE WITH GOD
It is imperative to be in tune with God and His agenda for your practices and ministry engagements. Although it is great to have a plan, there may be times where God will change the plan, and instead of dancing he may want the team to spend practice praying, receiving deliverance and healing, soaking and refreshing in him, and etc. There also may be times, where you will begin to prepare one dance, but God will change it, and give you a new dance to minister. Stay in tune with him and trust where he leads you.

Be open to continually asking God to give you His plan for practice and engagements. As he shares with you, remain open and flexible to flowing with him when he changes things. If you are not open and flexible to flowing in, God you will not hear from him, and you will miss what he is desiring for your practices and what he is desiring for you to minister.

Practice for dance ministers is much like a preacher preparing to deliver God's word. We practice and prepare to deliver God's word, just as a preacher studies and writes to deliver God's word. There are times where a preacher begins with one sermon and focus that God is giving, but then God may begin to lead him in another direction. The preacher begins to write this new word that God is releasing.

There is a purpose for why God began to give him another word. If he does not come into that plan and purpose, he risks
- The people not truly getting what they need
- The word falling on bad infertile ground
- Releasing a word outside of God's timing, where the people may not be in a place to receive
- His entire ministry being ineffective

The original word may have provided intercession for the new word. The original word could also be for a later date for when they people are in a posture to receive and be transformed by it. This is the same with dance ministers and ministries. The team may not be in a place at that moment to learn a lot of choreography. They may need that time for intercession, dissecting the word and refreshing in the Lord's presence. It is important that we are open and flexible to hearing and flowing with God's plan and agenda, such that practices and engagements are effective with his transformation power and sufficiency.

RELATIONSHIP & DISCERNMENT
As a dance leader, it is vital to discern what things may be oppressing or attacking your team members. There are times where the enemy will attack the members and you will be wondering what is going on with them. They may have trial in their live which is causing certain behaviors or it is a door opener to the attacks of the enemy. There could be no door openers, yet they are being targeted by demonic forces.

One way to grow in this area is to pray weekly for your team members individually in your personal time, or come early and pray before each member before practice. As you take this time to pray, God downloads revelations and strategies to you to help released oppression or attacks off your team. These things are annihilated and are not able to distract practices or engagements.

Taking this stance causes you to shift from a natural perspective and into a spiritual perspective. This alleviates frustration, anger, confusion, and division from occurring amongst your team, because you have dealt with the attacks spiritually. Having a spiritual perspective and not a natural one shifts you from becoming frustrated or angry with your team members when spirits are attacking them. From the natural eye, it may at times, look as though they are being lazy, they do not want to be there, they are distracted, they cannot pick up the movements and execute them correctly, but from the spiritual eye you can discern the truth and deal with the opposing forces as God leads.

There will not always be spirits attacking your team members. As a leader you should be in tune with your team members and have an individual relationship with each of them. Through this relationship, healthy communication, care, and love for one another can be cultivated. Your prayers and concern for them should also produce sight into who that dance minister is in God.

By cultivating a healthy communicative relationship you can be aware of the things that they may need prayer for, help with, edification in, and you will be able to understand and know why they may be dealing with certain things. You can pray with them, encourage, comfort, and build them up individually and as a team member. Never just rely on what you know about a team member, or what they have spoken to you, as familiarity can cause error and misperceptions to occur. Use your discernment as well as what was received through relationship, and be open to hearing from God directly about your team members. God will reveal things to you about them that are outside of your prior knowledge and give you grace to walk with them to wholeness. These relationships should include both you, the team member, and God, such that they are rooted in God's vision and plan for that person's life, your life, while embodying, the nature, character, and love of God in each of you individually and for the entire team.

> **1Thessalonians 5:11-13** *Wherefore comfort yourselves together, and edify one another, even as also ye do. And we beseech you, brethren, to know them which labour among you, and are over you in the Lord, and admonish you; And to esteem them very highly in love for their work's sake. And be at peace among yourselves.*

<u>Comfort</u> in the Strong's in this scripture means:
1. to call near
2. desire
3. pray
4. to address, speak to
5. instruct, admonish, exhort
6. to console, to encourage and strengthen by consolation

All of these words speak relationship. And it tells us to have healthy communication that addresses, speaks to, instructs, and admonishes. We are to have consoles that encourages and strengthens those who we are in relationship with.

The scripture says that we should know those who labor among us.

<u>Know</u> in the Strong's in this scripture means:
1. to see
2. to perceive with the eyes
3. to perceive by any of the senses
4. to perceive, notice, discern, discover

5. to pay attention, observe
6. to see something about
7. to have an interview with, to visit
8. to have regard for one, cherish, pay attention

Knowing those who you minister with also implies relationship as the definition describes it as having an interview and visit with them, paying attention to, cherishing, and showing concern for a person. Knowing also gives you sight and perception into who a person is, things that may attack and hinder them, and even revelation of inner personal things that may be going on. It causes your senses to open to discern, observe, notice, and discover things about them.

We also see in *1Thessalonians 5:13*, that as we come to know those who labor amongst us, we are to esteem, strengthen, edify, encourage and empower them intricately in love, for this will keep peace among us. Team relationships, and healthy communication are key to fulfilling the vision of the ministry and of each dance minister.

We charge you this day to God forth in God and allow him to empower your team as you thwart every plan of the enemy against you as a dance minister and your dance team. **SHIFT!**

CITATIONS

Definitions, Bible References, and Strong Concordance citations are from the following Sources:
1. *Dictionary.com*
2. *The Holy Bible from Olive Tree App & Biblegateway.com*
3. *Wikipedia*

Kingdom Shifters Books & Apparel
Available at Kingdomshifters.com

BOOKS FOR EVERYONE

Healing The Wounded Leader   Kingdom Shifters Decree That Thang

There Is An App For That   Kingdom Watchman Builder On the Wall

Embodiment Of A Kingdom Watchman   Dismantling Homosexuality Handbook
````` Releasing The Vision                Feasting In His Presence

Kingdom Heirs Decree That Thing           Let There Be Sight

Atmosphere Changers (Weaponry)

### BOOKS FOR DANCERS

Dancers! Dancers! Decree That Thang

Spirits That Attack Dance Ministers & Ministries

### TEE SHIRTS

Kingdom Shifters Tee Shirt                Let The Fruit Speak Tee Shirt

Releasing The Vision Tee Shirt            Kingdom Perspective Tee Shirt

Stand in Position Tee Shirt               No Defense Tee Shirt

My God Rules Like A Boss Tee Shirt        Destiny Blueprint Tee Shirt

### CD'S

Decree That Thing CD

Kingdom Heirs Decree That Thing CD

Teachings & Worship CD's
`````

www.ingramcontent.com/pod-product-compliance
Lightning Source LLC
Chambersburg PA
CBHW051932160426
43198CB00012B/2120